HEBREWS

ENCOURAGEMENT
FOR A LIFE OF FAITH

DALEN C. JACKSON

Annual
Bible
Study

Study Guide

SMYTH&HELWYS
PUBLISHING, INCORPORATED · MACON, GEORGIA

CONTENTS

Annual Bible Study

Cecil P. Staton, Jr.
President

David L. Cassady
Executive Vice President /
Publisher

Lex Horton
Vice President,
Editorial / Production

Mark K. McElroy
Senior Editor

P. Keith Gammons
Editor

Leslie Andres
Editorial Associate

Kelley F. Land
Assistant Editor

Barclay Burns
Vickie Frayne
Dave Jones
Graphic Design

Cover art
Menorah on synagogue door
(Credit: istockphoto.com)

1-800-747-3016 (USA)
1-800-568-1248 (Canada)

SMYTH&HELWYS
PUBLISHING INCORPORATED   MACON, GEORGIA
WWW.HELWYS.COM

ACKNOWLEDGMENTS

The author of Hebrews was clearly in the business of encouragement, and he stressed to his beleaguered readers the importance of provoking one another to good deeds and encouraging one another. I hope this study of Hebrews will be an encouragement to all who read it. I also hope the message meant for building up the faith of early believers will not be overshadowed by concerns for doctrinal precision on matters that were apparently not the author's primary focus.

In my own work of preparing these study materials, I benefited greatly from the encouragement of many, and I would like to acknowledge a few of those here. First, I am grateful to my wife Shari and my children Daniel and Emma for their forbearance through the months when my mind and energies were so largely devoted to this project.

I am especially thankful to the community of Baptist Seminary of Kentucky for the support and encouragement I received as I worked through Hebrews. President Greg Earwood has given unqualified support from the beginning, and my students have offered interest and enthusiasm in all of my classes and in many conversations through these months.

I am grateful as well to Smyth & Helwys Publishing and their commitment through the years to provide valuable Bible study resources for our churches. I appreciate the opportunity to contribute to this fine Annual Bible Study series, and I am sincerely thankful to Keith Gammons for his confidence in me and his guidance in editing my work.

Finally, I would like to express my deepest appreciation to my mother and father, whose support and encouragement not only for this project but for a lifetime of projects I cannot even begin to describe. Their queries about my progress (and good humor in the face of my frequent lack of progress) as I worked on this study, their tireless devotion to caring for all of our family, and the example they set by their faith and service to others have given me a lifetime of inspiration.

Dedicated to
Murl and Gwen Jackson,
through whose lives and love I have always known
the assurance of things hoped for,
the conviction of things not seen.

Chapter One

FACING CHALLENGES TO FAITH

Hope. Everyone needs hope to survive in this world. Some people play the lottery because it gives them hope that they might suddenly become wealthy beyond their wildest dreams, even though their chances of winning are less than their chances of being killed in an accident while driving to buy the ticket and home again. Most of us look hopefully toward small pleasures in our lives, times when we will be together with friends and family, vacations when we can see exciting places or experience the peacefulness of the beach or the mountains, the completion of a project that will give us at least a time of satisfaction. We work and plan and make sacrifices so that we will be able to realize these hopes, and the thought of the pleasure they will bring helps sustain us on difficult days.

But our world is often indifferent at best, and brutal at worst, toward our hopes. We all experience pain and suffering, the frustration of our good intentions and the corruption of our resolve to do good. Even as Christians, we sometimes lose sight of the faithfulness of God and the promise of God to make something good out of us and our world. Such was evidently the case with the original recipients of the letter to the Hebrews. They were so discouraged that they were dropping out of the community of believers and contemplating giving up on Christianity altogether. We don't know exactly who these Christians were or what problems they faced, but we can make informed guesses. They were devoted to the worship of the one God, through Christ, in a culture that worshiped many gods and saw these Christians as dangerous and antisocial because they refused to worship the local gods. Their closest cultural kin were the Jews, who also worshiped the one God, but they were even estranged from them because the Jews were offended by the Christians' insistence that God had come to earth in the person of Jesus. The Christians were tired of the struggle and losing sight of the hope that once sustained them.

The author of Hebrews knew, though, that within these Christians was a flame of faith that at one time burned brightly but now only smoldered and sputtered. He was determined to fan the flame, to encourage them to renew the hope that once made their lives vibrant in Christ. The letter we call Hebrews is the result of that effort. We don't know who the author was, or who the Christians were to whom he wrote. What we do know is that he crafted a colorful sermon full of images and arguments meant to persuade them to recommit themselves to Christ. In some parts of the sermon, his appeal goes beyond an explanation of *why* they should have faith; he gives them direct and personal challenges to get back on track with their worship of Christ and with living lives of love, hope, and service to others.

This first chapter will explore especially some of the more direct and personal words of the author of Hebrews to his readers. Hebrews is a letter in the sense that it was written down and sent to a distant group of people. It was probably to be read out loud in its entirety to the whole group upon arrival. It is also a sermon, carefully composed according to the best models of persuasive speaking in the ancient world. Within this framework, the sermon has several sections that stand out as direct encouragement, and chapter 1 focuses on these sections.

The letter of Hebrews has an introduction and a conclusion, both of which are intended to get the readers' attention and to help them begin to make connections between the information the letter conveys and their own lives. Between the introduction and conclusion, the main body of the letter, or sermon, is made up of three major sections in which the author lays out his argument. We sometimes refer to a formal argument of this sort as *exposition*, and I will use that term to designate the main sections that contain most of the author's explanations about God's faithfulness through Jesus and the reasons people should respond with faith. Each of these three sections of exposition is followed by a short digression in which the author again makes more personal appeals directly to the readers. I will refer to these sections as *exhortation*. So the outline of Hebrews looks something like this:

INTRODUCTION (1:1–2:9)

In the opening verses of the introduction, the author presents a strategy he uses throughout much of the letter, that of the comparison of earthly and historical approaches to relating to God with the new way available to all through faith in Jesus Christ. He begins by noting the ways people have received messages from God in the past. The prophets played a significant role in the Old Testament as spokespeople for God. They often prefaced their speeches with "Thus says the Lord." The message they brought to the people was indeed an important word from God. But the writer of Hebrews points out that the prophets still can't measure up to the very Son of God.

The same is true about angels. In numerous accounts from the Old Testament, angels came to people to relay a message from God or even to represent God in some way. People were often startled to realize that they had seen the angel of God, and their lives were always affected by their experience with the angel. Angels also announced the birth of Jesus as well as assurances to his followers at the empty tomb. Angels appeared to the first disciples who proclaimed the good news of Christ, protecting them and guiding them.

In our own time, angels are a source of great fascination. Bookstores have shelves of books about angels, and movies and television feature angels who penetrate the mundane world of our everyday existence, bringing supernatural wisdom and powers that reorient people to pay more attention to the power of God and the kind of lives God would have them lead. But the author of Hebrews says angels pale in comparison to this last messenger God has sent. This messenger *is* God.

Much of chapter 1 and the early verses of chapter 2 consist of quotes from the Old Testament in support of the assertion that Jesus is a messenger far superior to the angels. What is most notable about these Old Testament quotes is the way the author uses them as testimony about Jesus. You might never notice if you didn't look up these passages in the Old Testament, and even then you might not notice if you didn't study the passages carefully within their larger contexts. But if you did, perhaps you would notice that by using these Old Testament passages to refer to Christ, the author of Hebrews has found in each of them a meaning that probably would not have been evident to Jewish readers in the time before Christ.

This is not to say that Jewish readers would never have looked for multiple meanings in their Scriptures. In fact, the rabbis often did exactly that, and the style of interpretation we refer to as midrash frequently included reference to Scripture texts in creative ways that made those texts speak to new subjects to which they had not previously been applied. Why did the Jewish interpreters of that time and many of the early Christian interpreters feel free to interpret the sacred texts this way? For one thing, they evidently saw the texts as spiritual messages still alive with meaning, not as documents of value primarily as empirical evidence for the support of historical claims. These interpreters were products of a pre-modern world, a culture in which the rational scrutiny of our modern world would have been unimagined.

So the writer of Hebrews follows a well-worn tradition of interpretation in finding meanings in Old Testament passages that would not have occurred to the original Jewish recipients of those traditions. What *would* have distinguished his interpretation from that of the Jewish rabbis was his assertion that these passages represented testimony about *Jesus*. Throughout Hebrews, we will find references to the Old Testament interpreted in a fashion that could be characterized as *christocentric*. In other words, they all presume that the texts refer to Christ and that their meaning demonstrates God's message to Christians, even imbedded in Scriptures written hundreds of years before the time of Christ.

When Jewish readers read the words from Psalm 2:7, "You are my Son; today I have begotten you," they might well have thought of the kings of Israel and God's special protection over each leader of this chosen people. The larger context of Psalm 2 would suggest such a reading. However, when the author of Hebrews cites Psalm 2:7 in Hebrews 1:5, he does so assuming that these words are not about any earthly king of Israel, but about Jesus Christ. Likewise, the context of 2 Samuel 7:14, "I will be his father and he will be my son," would suggest the blessing of God on the descendents of David who would rule over Israel. But the author of Hebrews takes this statement and applies it explicitly and exclusively to Christ.

Through this manner of interpreting the Old Testament, the author of Hebrews puts together a formidable deposition from God, statement after statement demonstrating the superiority of Jesus to the angels. Because of the style of interpretation employed here, finding specifically Christian meanings where other meanings could easily be inferred, we cannot use these passages as *proof* in the modern sense of the nature of Christ. After all, this message was not intended to persuade people who had never made a commitment to following Christ. Instead, it was intended to reinforce the feelings of faith in those who already believed God had chosen to act through Jesus to bring salvation to the world. These interpretations of the Old Testament passages are not to be scrutinized, then, but rather to be celebrated. They are refrains that describe what Jesus means to us in earthly terms and images we can understand, even though we realize that the true glory of the nature of Christ is beyond our human imagination. Throughout the letter of Hebrews, we will encounter a multitude of such images, many adapted from Old Testament texts, that help us visualize and comprehend at least a shadow of the grace and majesty of God that was poured out to us through Christ.

The Main Themes of Hebrews

The introduction in many ancient speeches ends with a statement that summarizes the theme of the whole speech, and Hebrews seems to follow that convention. In Hebrews 2:5-9, the author makes the connection between this initial comparison of Jesus to the angels and the larger purpose of the sermon. Jesus is superior to the angels, but his coming to the earth is actually not about the angels at all. It's about people. As wonderful as angels seem, they really aren't a major part of God's plan for the world. God's plan is that people will someday have complete freedom to rule over the world, something even the angels will never have. Obviously, however, the world isn't like that yet. In this sense, people have been made "lower" than the angels for the time being, limited in this age by evil and sin that compromise them.

That's where Jesus comes in. Jesus didn't come to earth to do anything for the angels; he came to help people have a way to get from the present age in which they are captive to their own sin and the forces of evil to the point where they can receive God's promise of their freedom in the world to come. But in doing this, even Jesus had to become "lower" than the angels for a while, according to God's plan. So one of the main focal points of this sermon will be the illustration of what it meant for Jesus to lower himself so that he experienced the kind of human existence common to all people. The author of Hebrews will highlight the fact that Jesus experienced as much suffering and temptation as any person on earth could, and that by doing so Jesus became both like a brother to all people and like a high priest who could offer sacrifices on behalf of all people.

Another focal point of the sermon is the exaltation to which Jesus returned. He submitted willingly to the indignities of earthly life, to suffering and even to death, but it never conquered him. He endured the full extent of the powers of this age that hold people captive, but ultimately they held no power over him. By defying sin and death, Jesus defeated those powers and then returned to his position of exaltation. Hebrews returns again and again to images of Jesus, "crowned with glory and honor," waiting for the day when the world will finally be transformed from this age to the next.

These, then, are some of the main themes of Hebrews: Jesus lowered himself and became human; he defeated death and sin not for himself but on behalf of people; and he is once more exalted to glory where he waits for people to be glorified with him. The writer of Hebrews offers these themes in the context of encouragement to the recipients of the letter, or sermon. Jesus' faithfulness

Christ Enthroned

Jovan Vasilievic. 18th C. *Christ Enthroned.* Wood. Icon. Monastery, Krusedol, Serbia.

to people in lowering himself is not only meaningful because of what will happen at the end of this age, but it has enormous implications for the way people live their lives on earth even now. And Jesus' faithfulness demands a response of faithfulness on the part of people. Much of this sermon is meant to help people picture Jesus and his intercession on behalf of them so that they will be fortified to live out holy lives committed to the way of Jesus.

DIRECT EXHORTATION IN HEBREWS

While much of Hebrews consists of images and explanations that construct a coherent argument for how people should understand what Jesus has done and why people should respond with faith toward Christ, some major sections of the letter also challenge the readers to an immediate response on the basis of that argument. These sections are Hebrews 5:11–6:20, 10:26-39, and 12:25-27. These are not the only places where such direct appeals to the readers are made—sometimes the author makes similar, but brief, appeals in the middle of laying out the images and the explanations in his argument. But these sections seem to have the direct exhortation more as their focus and not so much as an aside. They also seem to be intentionally placed at strategic points after major sections of the arguments so that they provide a balance within the whole letter between exposition and exhortation.

In this study guide, it is possible to treat these three sections of exhortation in the same chapter because they are so similar to each other. Whereas the development of the argument, or the exposition, follows a train of thought that moves from one topic to the next and develops by means of a series of images systematically presented, the exhortation sections largely repeat the same kinds of warnings and encouragements. Some of these warnings and encouragements come in the form of direct commands, and the author uses the words "you" and "yours" frequently in these sections as he calls for his readers to examine their own lives. However, the author also frequently says "we" and "let us" as he includes himself in these exhortations. At all times, the sermon maintains the tone of a passionate and caring pastor offering words of hope to people he loves and for whom he wishes only the best.

First Exhortation (5:11–6:20)

The first major section of exhortation is found in Hebrews 5:11–6:20, and it is developed in three main sections. First, the author offers a fairly harsh critique of the state of the readers' faith and their lack of maturity (5:11–6:3). Second, he fashions a stern warning about the danger of falling away from faith (6:3-8). Finally, he expresses his confidence that they will stay on course and reassures them that the faithfulness of God is worthy of their continued faith (6:9-20).

5:11-6:3. First, the author takes his readers to task for failing to grow in their faith. They apparently have done well enough at learning the basic, foundational teachings, but accepting these teachings seems not to be a satisfactory fulfillment of faith itself. Many Christians today think the faith that leads to salvation primarily consists of holding a proper set of beliefs about their own sinful nature and about the death, resurrection, and second coming of Jesus. The author of Hebrews seems to see such beliefs as only the first stage in a fully developed faith.

6:4-8. The description of the readers' lack of maturity and failure to grow in faith gives way in these verses to a vivid warning about what will happen to them if they continue to drift without making a firm commitment to following the way of Christ. These verses have been a source of much contention among Christians, especially among Protestants, because the stark picture they paint of the possibility that people could lose their salvation is hard to reconcile with the understandings of salvation held by some people. How could it be that these people, who have accepted the basic beliefs about their own need to repent and about Jesus' death and resurrection and second coming, could lose their salvation and have no chance to be saved again?

Based on their interpretation of images found elsewhere in the New Testament, many Christians hold to a belief of "once saved, always saved." More formal doctrines referring to the "eternal security," or the "perseverance," of the believers lay the foundation for such a claim. Those doctrines are usually part of a larger system of doctrine, often emphasizing God's predestination (determining ahead of time) of who will be saved. Within such a system of doctrine, this warning in Hebrews would have to be interpreted in one of two ways. Either the people being addressed in this letter never truly had sufficient faith in the first place to be saved (so their falling away isn't a loss of salvation, which they never had) or God has predestined them to have faith and then lose it. The first of these views has a number of supporters, while probably only a few people would support the second today.

Many other Christians do not believe in the idea of "once saved, always saved." These Christians tend to put more emphasis on the role of people in choosing whether or not to commit themselves to faith in Jesus. For them, this warning is fairly straightforward. A person who has come to belief in Jesus and has claimed the promise of salvation can also choose to reject Jesus and suffer the loss of that salvation.

Another issue that plays a significant role in the interpretation of this warning is how a person understands the nature of faith that leads to salvation in the first place. Some believe salvation comes as the result of an instantaneous decision a person makes, a moment when that person affirms a belief in certain things *about* Jesus. Within evangelical Protestantism, this view has become increasingly popular over the last hundred years or so, accompanied by the emergence of a number of simple descriptions of the necessary beliefs (the "four spiritual laws," the "Romans road," the "plan of salvation," etc.). From this viewpoint, if the people addressed in Hebrews have indeed already made a "pro-fession of faith" in Christ, bringing about this instantaneous certainty of salvation, then the possibility of falling away would also seem likely to be based on an instantaneous decision to reject Christ.

Such a scenario is jarring, and it is difficult to imagine the circumstances that would lead a person to such an abrupt and final rejection of Christ. It also seems like a harsh and unforgiving punishment from a God who is notoriously slow to anger and quick to forgive. These sentiments probably lead many people to favor the view that the author of Hebrews is addressing people who have never truly made a sincere commitment to belief in Christ; they somehow have merely *seemed* to make that commitment, but their hearts have somehow not been completely behind it.

On the other hand, some Christians have a different understanding of the faith that leads to salvation. Instead of a momentary decision based on beliefs alone, they understand faith as a commitment to a pilgrimage of following Christ throughout one's life. In this understanding of faith, there is no one moment in which a person "receives Christ" and salvation is automatically granted. With this understanding of faith in mind, the warnings in Hebrews 6 would speak not to a momentary change of a person's mind, but rather to an intentional and persistent rejection of the way of Christ.

Honestly, numerous statements in the New Testament could support both of these understandings of the faith that leads to salvation. People who insist that one or the other understanding is the only correct understanding base their claim on traditions of interpretation that have developed out of human attempts to bring a satisfying unity to the Bible. Those traditions choose some passages to be interpreted more literally and taken more seriously than others. If we look at all the images in all the passages that speak of faith and salvation, we find in fact a mixed bag of descriptions.

What are Christians to do about these warnings in Hebrews? Reduce the issues to slogans that fit our own predispositions? Hit each other over the head with our doctrines and insist that our interpretations are unquestionably orthodox? These have been popular responses over the years. But is there a way beyond this impasse? Perhaps there is.

Some people will not be satisfied with answers that remain somewhat ambiguous, but in this case the original intention of the texts did not necessarily require doctrinal precision about the exact relationship between faith and salvation. After all, the writer of Hebrews was a pastor, writing out of pastoral concerns, not a systematic theologian. His reason for writing was his urgent desire to lead his beloved readers back to a vigorous and strong faith. His arguments as well as his direct warnings and encouragements were not to be dissected, but to stir the hearts and minds of these Christian brothers and sisters to commit themselves anew to following the way of Christ.

In light of this understanding of the purpose of Hebrews, maybe it is sufficient simply to say in terms of doctrine that God will judge those who claim to have faith. Regardless of what kind of experiences people may have that qualify them to be considered faithful, the author of Hebrews clearly calls every person to have a strong commitment to following the way of Jesus. We should have concern if we are not maturing in faith, and we should have some fear of how we will be judged before God if we are not. The images found in the letter, then, do not constitute a rulebook to be studied for doctrine but a passionate vision to be read for inspiration and motivation.

6:9-20. The final verses of this section of exhortation are as affirming as the previous verses are threatening. The author expresses his confidence that those to whom he writes are indeed on the right track toward a faith that gives them reason to have hope. His confidence is based in part on his understanding of the fairness of God. Notice that in assuring his readers of God's fairness, he points out that God will take into consideration the good works and compassion they have shown. Does this mean that salvation is based in part on works? This, again, is a statement that does not fit neatly into the understanding of faith and salvation held by some Christians, but it demonstrates the complexity and the mystery of the whole process of God's granting of salvation by grace.

While the author expresses confidence in the faith of his readers, his hope for their salvation is based even more on what he knows about the faithfulness of God. He is sure of the fairness of God because he knows that is an important part of God's character, but in 6:13-20 he also appeals to God's faithfulness based on the story of God's constant commitment to Abraham and his heirs. God makes promises and keeps those promises. God's word is good, so good that the author can refer to the hope based on God's word as an "anchor of the soul."

Second Exhortation (10:19-39)

The second major section of exhortation, in 10:19-39, follows a lengthy section of argument that develops the role of Jesus as high priest and highlights the importance of the shedding of Jesus' own blood. The author briefly summarizes these images in the first verses of the exhortation, showing again that because of God's faithfulness, Christians can have confidence to make a commitment to God. As in the previous exhortation, the author uses "we" and "let us" as frequent reminders that he is not simply giving orders but instead shares with his readers in both the blessings and the hardships of Christian discipleship. In this section of exhortation, the encouraging affirmation comes first, and no statements in the whole letter are more affirming. Verse 23 captures the essence of the whole sermon in its intent to encourage: "Let us hold fast to the confession of our hope without wavering, for he who has promised is faithful."

This unqualified call to faith is followed immediately by practical implications. The readers of this letter are already wobbly in their faith, so they will need to support one another to find the strength to "hold fast." They should consider how to bring out the best in each other, to encourage love and good deeds. Apparently some of them had been taking community gatherings for granted, and the author urges them to make the most of such opportunities. This urging comes across not as a legalistic concern about church attendance but as wise pastoral advice for Christians who need each other's support in their struggles.

This positive encouragement gives way, however, to another stern warning about the dangers of rejecting faith in Christ after some initial acceptance. The images are as threatening as in the previous section of exhortation, and the exact nature of the faith in question is equally ambiguous. The situation of the people in danger of rejecting faith in this hypothetical scenario is that they have "received the knowledge of the truth" (10:26), "were sanctified" by the blood of the covenant (10:29), and "had been enlightened" (10:32). So this passage again raises the question of the exact status of their faith.

Once again, however, this dire warning gives way to pleading that reminds the readers of their previous faithfulness and encourages them to return to their earlier ways. The description of the faithful ways they once followed does not refer to doctrines they professed, but to good deeds they did. Reminders of these good deeds are mingled together in 10:32-39 both with assurances of God's promises and with warnings about God's judgment on those who "shrink back." If we take this whole section of exhortation seriously, we must examine our lives and see what kinds of deeds we are doing that demonstrate our faith in Christ.

One other current that runs through this section and much of the letter of Hebrews is an apocalyptic perspective. This is a consciousness of the approaching time when God will bring about a sudden end to the present age. The end of the present age will lead to a transformation of the earth and a time of judgment and reward for all people. Many Jewish writings over several centuries had depicted such scenarios by the time Hebrews was written, and the early Christians were deeply influenced by this way of thinking. The reference in 10:37 to the one who is coming "in a very little while" reflects the influence of this tradition. While the author of Hebrews sees Christ's sacrifice as a victory of God that already has a transforming effect on the lives of Christians in the present time, this future perspective offers the complete fulfillment of the hopes and promises that are not yet apparent.

Third Exhortation (12:25-27)

The final section of exhortation, 12:25-27, is brief, but it contains the same kind of direct warning we have seen in the other two, as well as the same apocalyptic perspective. These verses evoke the shaking of earth and heaven, with the result that only heaven remains. The warning is pointed and clear: "See that you do not refuse the one who is speaking." And "the one who is speaking" refers to Jesus, who spoke by shedding his blood (12:24).

THE CONCLUSION OF HEBREWS

Hebrews 12:28–13:25 makes up the conclusion of the letter. In these verses, the author makes a final appeal to his readers on the basis of the argument he has constructed in the sermon. This appeal seems to be intended primarily as a call to action for the readers. Once more, it is instructive that the author does not summarize doctrines the readers should embrace. Neither does he call for them simply to profess their belief in Jesus. Instead, he offers suggestions as to how they might live out their faith. Is this a comprehensive list of what Christians must do to show faith? That's unlikely. It probably merely reflects some of the most important needs in the community to which the letter was written and some of the ministries for which the author knew his readers were gifted and called to carry out.

In 12:28, on the basis of the fact that God has granted to them "a kingdom that cannot be shaken," the author calls his readers to offer thanks to God in the form of "an acceptable worship with reverence and awe." The instructions for faithful deeds follow immediately, so it is not unreasonable to conclude that the "acceptable worship" to which he refers is in fact the living out of their faith by doing these deeds. Remember that in his earlier exhortations he urged them to "go on toward perfection" (6:1), and he expressed his confidence that they would do the "better things . . . that lead to salvation" (5:9). These instructions for works of faith in the conclusion seem to provide more concrete instructions as to how they might do those things. None of the deeds listed should be surprising to any of us, but many of them are also easy to overlook in our busy lives. Perhaps it would be valuable for all Christians to review this list from time to time to help us think once again about the lives God calls us to live as people who have faith in the "unshakable" kingdom that Jesus died to make available to us.

Sisterly, Brotherly Love (13:1)

The New Revised Standard Version says "mutual love" here, probably in an attempt to avoid the unnecessarily exclusive "brotherly love" of some other translations. But the kind of love siblings have for one another is in view here, and the author argues in one of his sections of exposition that Jesus himself showed brotherly love in his human life. We should evaluate the kinds of relationships we have with one another in our churches against this standard.

Hospitality (13:2)

We live in a dangerous world, and unfortunately we have to be as wise as serpents when it comes to offering kindness to strangers. Still, God calls us to find ways to welcome people who need access to the most basic necessities of life. We may have to be creative to do so, and we may have to work together within our church or even among several churches, but we should never lose sight of this calling. Exactly who are these strangers? We don't know all the circumstances surrounding the early Christians, or where such strangers would have come from. But everyone we do not know is a candidate. And some of them might be angels.

Remembering Those in Prison (13:3)

This instruction clearly goes back to traditions about Jesus' own teaching. It stands opposed to the neat boundaries most of us construct in our minds that divide the good people from the bad people. It is easy in our culture to avoid even thinking about those who are in prison. We don't see them, we don't hear about them; we have effectively removed them from our lives. But their lives are important to God.

Honorable Marriage (13:4)

Faithfulness in marriage relationships and sexual purity for all Christians are the focus of this instruction. Whether the early Christians carried these values over from Judaism, surmised them from currents within the Greco-Roman culture, or saw them as unique demonstrations of holiness fitting for followers of Christ, they were consistently seen as essential elements of Christian living.

Avoiding the Love of Money (13:5-6)

This instruction has been even more subject to cultural accommodation than any instructions about sexuality, especially in the western world, but biblical literalists seldom target it for protest. Those who ignore this instruction (and the numerous similar statements throughout the Bible) typically can do so with impunity and remain in good standing in our churches. In fairness, market economies such as ours do demand that we weigh the intention of this instruction and consider how we might carry it out within our culture. But we must not ignore it, and we must be open to treating biblical instructions about other issues similarly. In doing so, we should always be alert to our own self-interest, but self-interest can be the basis for denying important adaptations of biblical instructions as well as for accepting accommodation too freely.

Follow the Leaders (13:7-8)

The previous instructions make up the first block of material in chapter 13, and this verse starts a second block, which both begins and ends with instructions concerning the leadership of the Christian readers of Hebrews. Keep in mind that the early Christians did not yet have any distinctively Christian Scriptures to guide them. Imitating the earliest leaders was their best way of learning about living the Christian life. The author of Hebrews undoubtedly had a special relationship with the Christians to whom he wrote, and he knew their leaders and those leaders' worthiness for imitation. He also reminds the people that beyond those leaders, they can rely on the example of Jesus Christ, who never changes.

Strange Teachings and Acceptable Sacrifices (13:9-16)

This instruction also seems to relate to a particular situation the readers faced, perhaps having to do with the sacrifice of animals. While the exact circumstances are unknown to us, the resulting instruction is clear enough: the sacrifice that is acceptable to God is to praise God, confess the name of God, and do good works and share, even if doing these things brings persecution.

Follow the Leaders, Again (13:17)

As before, this instruction seems to assume both the writer's familiarity with and his confidence in the leadership of those to whom he writes. Obedience to leaders is important for the spiritual formation of individuals as well as for the health of a community of faith. However, dissent has also proven to be healthy for the church all too frequently. We must be on guard for the corruption that plagues even many of our respected leaders, who, after all, are only human.

Final Thoughts (13:18-25)

The sermon closes with a request for prayer by the author and a benediction that pulls together many of the prominent themes of the sermon. Some final appeals and instructions round out the letter itself.

EXHORTATION IN HEBREWS

As a whole, the letter of Hebrews is more than anything a call to faithfulness for its readers. The following chapters of this study guide address the arguments laid out by the author of Hebrews as to why the readers should be faithful. Those arguments are important, but we must not lose sight of their context and their intention. They are presented to help provoke readers to do the things they should do. At places we will do a disservice to the text if we press the analogies and images too hard in an attempt to make them all fit together neatly as a systematized body of doctrine. The sections we have examined in this chapter highlight the author's constant concern throughout the letter for the readers' commitment to following Christ. And that commitment calls for them to live out their faith in an active way. The author never presents his arguments as beliefs that must be guarded carefully and professed accurately; he presents them as the grounds for action.

STUDY QUESTIONS

1. In what ways is Hebrews a letter, and in what ways is it a sermon?

2. Why do you think the author of Hebrews puts such a heavy emphasis on the divinity of Jesus in the introduction to Hebrews? What do you think are some of the most important implications of Jesus being "truly God"?

3. Why do you think the author of Hebrews compared Jesus to angels? How is Christ superior to angels?

4. What is the relationship between Jesus' exaltation to glory and his suffering? Between people's exaltation to glory and their suffering?

5. What do you think are signs in the contemporary church of Christians "relying on milk" for nourishment instead of "solid food"? What are characteristics of Christians who have moved on to "solid food"?

6. How has your tradition helped shaped your understandings of predestination and free will and about the possibility of people losing their salvation?

7. What do you think the author of Hebrews would say about modern controversies over whether salvation can be lost?

8. Do you understand the faith that leads to salvation as something that comes in a moment of decision, something lived out over a lifetime, or something else?

9. Which is more persuasive to you, the encouragement in Hebrews or the warnings?

10. What are the characteristics of a life of faith?

FOR INDIVIDUAL STUDY

If you are using this book to study Hebrews apart from a study group, start out your study of this section by observing how it fits into the larger development of the sermon. The passages addressed in this section provide a framework for the letter as a whole by providing an introduction, a conclusion, and exhortation sections that alternate with the exposition, or argument, in the letter. Look through the pages of Hebrews and familiarize yourself with where these sections are and how they fit with the rest of the letter. The study prompts above should give you additional guidance for focusing on the important ideas in this section.

Chapter Two

THE SIGNIFICANCE
OF CHRIST

In this chapter, we will examine the first of the sections in Hebrews that presents the argument for why readers should continue to follow Christ. There are three such sections, and the argument, or exposition, of the letter unfolds across these sections as images and stories and explanations. The first section is found in 2:10–5:10. In it, the author develops several different images of Christ along with images of the unsuccessful results of God's offer to give help to Israel in a previous age.

The images, stories, and explanations in this section are woven together; they don't lay out an argument step by step, building one upon the other as we would typically build an argument in our modern western culture. The result has some similarities to a quilt, a tapestry, or a collage, to make comparisons to these visual media. We can focus on individual themes that run through the argument, and they each make statements about such things as the faithfulness of God or the characteristics of Jesus' saving actions or Israel's response to God. But all of them as a whole make up the argument of the sermon. The sermon cannot be reduced to a series of facts or beliefs, and neither can any of the themes represented by the images, stories, and explanations.

For this reason, I have chosen not to try to choose two or three representative passages from Hebrews or even from each section to demonstrate the essence of the letter. The essence of the letter is its dramatic quality, its vivid display of illustrations that offer an emotional appeal to the reader to forsake all else and follow Christ. I will try to survey these various images, stories, and arguments so that you can read through them all with the idea of taking in the whole effect they create. Imagine that the author of Hebrews could put together a multimedia presentation to show his readers why they should recommit themselves to following Christ. Within the limits imposed on a spoken sermon that must be written down and read, that is what Hebrews is.

The argument of this section of Hebrews is presented in what amounts to roughly three different scenarios. The first, in 2:10-18, describes how fitting it was for God to send Jesus to suffer so that he could become like a brother to all the people on earth, who also suffer. The second section, in 3:1–4:13, revolves around the image of God's offer of rest to the Israelites and the status of that offer for people "today" since Israel rejected it. The third section, in 4:14–5:10, explores the image of Jesus as the high priest, comparing and contrasting him to the earthly high priests.

A FITTING SON AND BROTHER (2:10-18)

Here in 2:10 and again in 7:26, the author declares that Jesus is a *fitting* answer to the needs of people. In this instance, that is because of the suffering Jesus underwent. His suffering was not a given, not something to which God had to subject Jesus. God's intention was to bring people to glory, but people were subject to suffering and testing and the power of death. So the fitting solution was to send a son to be exposed to the same kind of suffering and testing and death.

One result was that Jesus developed a kind of solidarity with people, becoming like a brother to them. Who better, then, to square off against the powers that hold people captive than our "brother"? There is no fully logical explanation for how God could become a brother to people or how a brother could vicariously defeat these forces on behalf of people, and yet it seems most natural and quite intuitive when the author of Hebrews makes the argument. Perhaps there is no precedent, no rule that says this is how it must be, but there can be no question that at some primitive level, it seems fitting. Through much of the rest of the argument in Hebrews, the author will continue to use imagery to describe Jesus that corresponds to the characteristics we would expect of a brother watching out for his siblings.

Another term the author uses to describe Jesus in 2:10 is "pioneer." This refers to someone who does things that have not been done before, who leads the way in accomplishing something that will benefit others who are to follow. The readers of this letter had probably heard many different kinds of stories about heroes, but never one like this one. Jesus came from a more exalted place than any Greek god or Jewish holy man. And yet he was willing to get his hands dirty with the business of regular people. Even so, when he found himself in the form of a regular person, he did things no other person had ever been able to do. He explored a frontier that took him through the territories of sin and death, and he staked a claim there that entitled all people who would trust him to pass freely and unharmed through those territories. Jesus was indeed a pioneer of faith and of victory over sin and death. His life was a fitting response from God not only because he was like the people he came to save, but also because he was able to rise above those people and accomplish the things that needed to be accomplished to lead them out of their predicament.

Jesus would not have been the fitting answer if God's concern were to save angels. A human could not have been a brother to angels, to show solidarity with them, nor could he have been a pioneer in some area that angels struggled to master. And so the earthly form of Jesus was fitting for his mission. It is difficult for us to imagine how God could become human, and the early church wrestled with how to understand the humanity of Jesus. In the end, though, the view that Jesus was fully human prevailed. And rightly so, because only in a fully human form could Jesus have truly and completely confronted the difficulties that plague people.

Keep in mind that both of these images of Jesus, brother and pioneer, operate at a spiritual level, and they were not characteristics people could necessarily have seen from his earthly life. People could have observed his goodness, and they certainly witnessed the death he suffered. But he was not physically a brother to all the people who followed him, and the way he redefined family as all those who do the will of God could only have been taken metaphorically. But as the argument develops in Hebrews, we will come to understand that a metaphor like this is a vehicle for deeper spiritual truths. The crucifixion of Jesus would not have been understood by those who witnessed it as a triumph over sin and death (although the resurrection would have made this a little more obvious for those who believed in it). But Hebrews calls us to see the suffering man on the cross as a pioneer, one who was entering uncharted territory by means of his suffering.

The author of Hebrews frequently appeals to verses from the Old Testament to support and illustrate his developing argument. Sometimes the verses he quotes come from passages that lend themselves to an obvious connection with the story of Jesus. More often, though, these verses seem to have one clear meaning related to the context of the Old Testament passage in which they are found and another, different meaning related to the images for Jesus that are found in Hebrews. Here in 2:12-14, the author appeals to verses from Psalm 22:22 and Isaiah 8:17-18 as witnesses supporting his argument. In their original contexts, these would seem to be the words of the psalmist and the prophet, respectively, but here in Hebrews they proclaim the message of Jesus related to his role as both Son of God and brother to humans.

In Hebrews 2:10-18, the images of pioneer and brother, with the support of the testimony from the Old Testament that voices Jesus' own perspective, all come together to begin to shape a vision of the faithfulness of God. The argument is not made up of logical proofs, but rather of powerful illustrations. The author no doubt intended that the readers would be persuaded by these images and moved to recommit themselves to following Christ. And this part of the author's vision of the faithfulness of God is based on an understanding of how God was willing to become human and be subject to awful things in order to bring about good things for all other humans. Surely this would strike a nerve with the Christians to whom the letter is addressed who were weighed down by the suffering they experienced.

And hopefully it begins to give us ideas about what it meant for God to become human. To what can we compare Jesus so that we can understand what his life was

Crucifixion

Jacopo Tintoretto. 1518–1594.
Crucifixion, detail of center section.
1565. Scuola Grande di San Rocco,
Venice, Italy.

about? A brother? A pioneer? Both of these images help us grasp the humanness of Christ. And they help us think about his relationship to us. Jesus did not come to be a distant stranger who battled evil forces. He came to help all the people who are enslaved to those forces. Jesus also didn't come to do anything that had ever been done before. It was a new thing he did, something no one had even quite imagined. This new thing (hence, the good *news*) expressed God's love and God's willingness to make something good out of people that fit those people better than any approach God had taken in the past.

In 2:17, the author introduces another role that will be important in envisioning the significance of Jesus. If the images of brother and pioneer help show how Jesus was fitting, how Jesus was able to confront temptation and even death on behalf of people, the image of Jesus as high priest helps show how Jesus acted as a mediator between people and God. This image of Jesus as high priest will be developed at length in the letter, both later in this first argument (in 4:14–5:10) and in the second major section of argument (in 7:1–8:5), but it is merely introduced here.

THE FAITHFULNESS OF CHRIST (3:1–4:13)

This second development of the first major section of argument in Hebrews presents a whole new set of images. But instead of providing descriptions that help us understand the humanity of Jesus, these verses conjure up a story and the actions of God in the past, present, and future. Actually, in 3:1-10, there is one more image of Jesus to set the stage for the next scenario. It involves the comparison of Jesus to Moses. Just as the whole letter began with comparisons between Jesus and prophets and angels, now the writer points out that Jesus was faithful like Moses, but worthy of more honor. The author offers a couple of analogies that once again do more to illustrate than to provide a logical proof. These analogies are tied together playfully by reference to the word "house," with the overall claim that Jesus is faithful over "all God's house" (3:2). First, Jesus has more honor than Moses the way a builder has more honor than the house that is built (3:3-4). And second, Jesus' faithfulness within God's house was more like that of a Son, whereas the faithfulness of Moses was more like that of a servant.

These comparisons of Jesus and Moses draw attention to the faithfulness of Jesus, which is offered to the readers as a reason for confidence and hope that they might receive from God what the followers of Moses never received. The following verses, all the way from 3:7 to 4:11, allude to a scene out of the wilderness experience of the Israelites in which they lost an opportunity to receive a great blessing from God. In these verses, two words become catchwords that tie the whole section together and also connect the ancient lost opportunity of the Israelites with a live opportunity for those who would follow Christ. Those words are "today" and "rest."

"Today" and "rest" happen to be the first and last words of a passage from Psalm 95:7-11 that the author quotes here. This psalm praises God as king, but it also urges the hearer to avoid the example of the Israelites in the wilderness. It calls for the hearer to listen to the voice of God "today," unlike the Israelites who hardened their hearts and tested God, even though they had seen the miracles God had performed on their behalf. The author of Hebrews offers the words of this psalm in the same spirit as the psalmist, urging his readers to avoid the stubbornness of the Israelites. For him the "today" of the psalmist becomes the "today" of his writing of this letter. As we read this letter of Hebrews, that "today" becomes the day we read and study and try to learn from the message of the letter.

Along with the word "today," the author picks up on the final words he quotes from the psalm. Because the Israelites' hearts have turned away from God, God is angry and promises, "They shall not enter my rest." So this word, "rest," becomes another keyword that allows the author to tie several variations on the word to the story of God's faithfulness to Israel. The whole of 3:12–4:11, then, consists of images highlighted by the words "today" and "rest," although those words will refer to a number of different things in the course of this short section. In fact, using these words to refer to different things is at the heart of the artistry of the passage. Ancient readers delighted in clever plays on words, and the author of Hebrews provides one here, not merely to dazzle the reader, but to move the reader to be persuaded by the results of the wordplay.

So the author, having reminded the readers of the psalm with its command for "today," calls them to "exhort one another every day, as long as it is called 'today'" (3:13). In this way, the "today" of the psalmist becomes the "today" of the writer of Hebrews and his readers. Then the author refers back to the psalm and clarifies the situation of the rebellion that the psalm mentions. It was the Israelites under Moses who rebelled as they wandered in the wilderness and were disobedient because of their unbelief (3:16-19). These are the ones at whom God was angry and who were forbidden to enter God's "rest."

With the beginning of chapter 4, the author makes the inference that if God didn't allow the Israelites to enter that rest, then entering that rest must still be available to someone. And he tells his readers that they themselves are eligible if they respond to God in faith. The author seems to recognize a need to explain this assertion further, and in 4:3-11 he develops a fairly complicated explanation, still centered on the words "rest" and "today." He begins by referring to God's "rest" on the seventh day after creating the world. As if someone might assume that once the seventh day was over, this special kind of rest would never come to anyone again, the author answers that since God told the Israelites they would not enter "my rest," there must have still been the possibility of people entering it. And when the psalmist spoke of the Israelites' failure and warned his listeners to avoid their example "today," there must have been yet another opportunity for people to enter God's rest.

The author of Hebrews sums up this argument by stating plainly that "rest" is still available to the people of God (today), a kind of Sabbath rest that allows them to "cease from their labors" (4:9-10). The whole argument seems a little convoluted, but it was exactly what the readers needed to hear. They were weary from the struggles they faced as they tried to maintain their faithfulness to following the way of Jesus. Rest was a welcome thought, and these images from the Old Testament wove together a promise of rest rooted in God's own Sabbath rest and available to all who continue in faith.

As we read these words today, we should be comforted by the images as well. The "today" of the psalmist or the writer of Hebrews should be no different than the "today" each day brings to us. We, too, can learn from the example of the Israelites that the failure to respond to God is disastrous. And we, too, can envision the "rest" God claimed at creation that can be a haven for us in a world of restlessness and trouble. For those who have never made a commitment to following God, the letter of Hebrews offers an invitation to make that commitment "today." For those who have already made a commitment, this letter is a reminder that "today" is no time to give up or to neglect to live the kind of life worthy of the sacrifice of Jesus.

As with much of the letter, this image based on "today" and "rest" is a mixture of warning and encouragement, but the verses that follow focus powerfully on first warning, then the encouragement. In 4:12-13, we find a harsh image of the judgment of God, presumably explaining the Israelites' failure to enter God's rest that has been discussed just before. Verse 11 ends the previous discussion of Psalm 95 with a final admonition to the readers to "make every effort to enter that rest, so that no one may fall through such disobedience as theirs [the Israelites']." Verse 12 follows with a stark description of the judging role of the word of God.

The description of the word of God here as "living and active, sharper than any two-edged sword, piercing until it divides soul from spirit, joints from marrow" has unfortunately been subjected to an interpretive tradition that frequently takes it out of this context and makes it a statement about Scripture. Scripture may well have these qualities as its inspired message intersects the lives of its readers at various points. But the reference here seems much more naturally to apply to God's message to the Israelites that they would not enter God's rest because of their disobedience and lack of faith. It is a message of judgment and a reminder that even though God is a God of great compassion, the character of God also includes a terrifying insistence on justice.

From a theological standpoint, this whole set of images presents an interesting and challenging view of the kind of faith that is necessary for salvation. Keep in mind that the author develops these images for the purpose of encouraging the ongoing faith of his readers. It is possible that the persuasive power of the images is their most important aspect and that the details they offer should not be pressed too literally. But Protestant churches tend to look to statements in texts like this to find information that can be used to develop doctrine. In that case, we cannot overlook the statement in 4:14 that seems to be at the heart of the author's instructions to his readers about what they must do to avoid the fate of the ancient Israelites: "For we have become partners of Christ, if only we hold our first confidence firm to the end." This statement does not fit well with an understanding of faith that calls for a one-time statement of belief as sufficient for salvation. It seems instead to require a lifetime commitment to following Christ.

Keep in mind, however, that the purpose of the writer of these words was to provoke his readers to a renewal of their faith. The frightening image of the rejection of Israel by God because of her lack of disobedience is intended to prod the recipients of this letter to persevere in following the way of Christ and maintaining the fellowship of the Christian community. It may be that the author was less concerned with the doctrinal implications of his statements than with the effect they would have on the readers. The image of Israel's rejection is in fact balanced by the hopeful word that "today" is a day of opportunity. This does not appear to be a message directed at those who have never heard of Christ, but rather it is an invitation to those who have already followed Christ but who have grown weary along the way. So our doctrinal categories are challenged consistently by these images, and yet the message is in many ways a simple one. The readers are to go back to living lives shaped by the transforming knowledge of Jesus.

JESUS THE HIGH PRIEST (4:14–5:10)

The final development of this section of the argument of Hebrews begins to present the image of Jesus as the great high priest. In this comparison, Jesus is still looked at as a human person, but as a very special person. This image of Jesus as high priest is perhaps the most distinctive image of Jesus in the letter to the Hebrews. Nowhere else in the New Testament besides in the book of Hebrews is Jesus referred to as a high priest. We should understand this image not as a description of the earthly role or actions of Jesus but as a figurative description of Jesus that puts into perspective the significance of his life.

The author has described Jesus as a high priest in passing in both 2:17 and 3:1, but it is not until 4:14 that he begins to indicate what the significance of this comparison might be. In the verses that follow, he will make at least three important assertions about Jesus related to the role of a high priest. First, Jesus is able to sympathize with human weakness. Second, he was tested but did not sin. And third, he assumed the role of priest not because he decided in any human way to do so, but because God called him to this service.

Underlying all of these assertions, of course, are basic understandings about what a high priest would have done and would have meant in the eyes of the early Christians. The author of Hebrews does not make these explicit, but we can make guesses based on what we know both about the high priests of the Jews and about priests in general in the Greco-Roman culture of which these early Christians found themselves a part. The role of priests of all sorts was to lead in the performance of rituals offered as worship to a god. Priests were seen to have a special ability to make sure the offerings got from the people to the god. So while they were still understood to be regular people at some level, in some sense they were also mediators with the gods, possessed of an extra measure of holiness that allowed them to approach nearer to the gods.

The frequent reference to the Jewish temple system in the letter to the Hebrews has led many through the years to presume that the recipients of the letter were Jewish themselves and were intimately associated with the Jewish priests and their role in Jewish worship at Jerusalem. We cannot be sure of this, but we do know that the earliest preachers of the gospel typically made frequent references to the traditions and writings of the Jews. Since temples for various gods were scattered throughout the ancient world, it would not have taken a great deal of imagination for the early Christians to envision the temple of the Jews in Jerusalem, whether or not they had seen the temple or been a part of worship there. And they would not have required a great deal of information about the role of the priests, or even the high priest, in order to grasp the comparisons the writer of Hebrews was making between Jesus and the high priest. In fact, the author provides the details necessary for making the connections he wants to highlight at each point of the way.

So in 4:14, the author begins by reminding his readers that this high priest is in at least one regard completely unlike any high priest of the Jewish temple or any other temple in this world—Jesus the high priest has passed through the heavens! Some of the images of Jesus we have seen already in this letter have emphasized his exaltation, the fact that he ascended into heaven and sits at the right hand of God. It is this exalted state of Jesus that makes his willingness to become human so extraordinary, and it also provides assurance that the forces of this world are no match for the power of God to overcome them. The writer offers this reminder, then, as grounds for confidence. "Since" we have such a high priest, "let us hold fast to our confession."

So the image of Jesus as high priest blends elements of the humanly characteristics of a high priest with the attributes that only the incarnate God could possess. As in the earlier part of this section, however, much of the emphasis is on the human experience of Christ both in comparison and in contrast with the high priestly figure. It is reasonable for us to assume that the author expects his readers to draw on their knowledge both of the earthly high priests and of the earthly life of Jesus in recognizing the bond that Jesus developed with them by the way he lived and died.

In 4:15, we can't help getting the impression that the readers might have found it hard to relate to earthly priests, seeing them as distant and insulated from the concerns more common people faced from day to day. If they were acquainted with the Jerusalem priesthood, we indeed might expect them to feel this way. The Jerusalem high priests, indeed virtually all of the priests, were members of the aristocracy. During the time of Jesus as well as in the formative years of the church, the priesthood had become highly political, influenced greatly by the Herod family and often tainted by bribes and other kinds of corruption. While the masses still tended to be supportive of the office of high priest, and from time to time the high priests took courageous stands in the interest of the Jews, the social and economic distance between the high priests and the people was substantial.

So when the author of Hebrews says in reference to Jesus that "we do not have a high priest who is unable to sympathize with our weaknesses," he may be touching on some of the deep-seated resentment toward high priests that resided even in the minds of people who identified positively with Judaism. How easily, then, the contrast with Jesus emerges. Jesus was never an aristocrat, one of the elite, but instead he had a reputation for associating with people from all walks of life, even those considered dishonorable by some of the Jews. It stands to reason that Jesus also experienced the same kinds of struggles and temptations as these people with whom he shared his time and, ultimately, his life.

A good illustration of this kind of sympathy attributed to Jesus might be seen in the life of the late pope John Paul II. At his death, great crowds gathered to honor him, and people around the globe joined in celebrating this life that had touched so many. And the stories of those who held him in such high regard returned over and over again to his simple roots in Poland and the humble and earnest interest he showed in each and every person he met.

Likewise, the stories of Jesus emphasized his humble roots and his lifestyle of compassion for even "the least of these." The author of Hebrews does not retell any of these stories, but we can assume that they provided the backdrop for this image of Jesus as a high priest who "in every respect has been tested as we are."

In one respect, however, Jesus is different from us and from all of those people with whom he associated during his lifetime. He was tested just as all of us are, "yet without sin." The thought of Jesus experiencing life as we do is both satisfying and comforting; the thought of him living that life without ever sinning is astounding and incredible. We have no frame of reference for even beginning to think about a perfect life—no pope, no evangelist, no missionary, not even a humble servant of the church whose life has been dedicated to prayer. But even if we cannot imagine such a life, we can appreciate its significance for what it says about the triumph of God over the powers of this world. The author of Hebrews was writing to people who were burdened not only by the persecution they experienced within the community around them, but also by their own powerlessness to overcome the temptations of the world. The victory of Christ over sin, especially because he faced the temptations common to all people, becomes a unique symbol of hope for everyone who struggles with such a burden.

The author of Hebrews presents this "priesthood" of Jesus as a basis for people to "approach the throne of grace with boldness" (4:16). If the role of a high priest is to mediate between the people and their God, Jesus has fulfilled that role to perfection. He has provided a direct line of appeal from people to God so they can "receive mercy and find grace to help in time of need." What a powerful message for Christians who were floundering between faith and despair. And who of us ever has enough mercy and grace in our lives? But through Jesus, we are able to ask God every day, any time, for more.

Chapter 5 continues the development of this image of Jesus as high priest, and here again Jesus is both compared to the best virtues of a high priest and contrasted with the shortcomings of all high priests who are merely human. Verse 1 emphasizes the mediating role of all high priests. Every high priest is in the business of offering gifts and sacrifices to God on behalf of people; from a religious standpoint, that is what is at the heart of being a high priest. And to some degree, the author of Hebrews concedes, all high priests have some ability to "deal gently with the ignorant and wayward" because of their own humanity (5:2). But for all earthly priests, the human weakness that allows them to empathize with people is also a liability. It means that they not only have to mediate with God on behalf of those people who come to them, but they have to mediate with God on their own behalf as well.

It seems that the need for an earthly high priest to offer sacrifice for himself should not be a significant impairment to his ability to offer sacrifice for everyone else. But keep in mind that the writer of this letter is pulling out all the stops to persuade his readers of the advantages of following Christ. Actually, this argument should be quite appealing to Americans, with our excessive interest in the value of efficiency. We hire efficiency experts to help us get the most out of our industries and businesses, and so it probably makes sense to us to get out the stopwatch and develop an assessment for the high priest. And this evaluation is a no-brainer. If the earthly high priests have to spend part of their time and energy offering sacrifice for their own sins, there is no way they can compare to Jesus, whose sacrifice is dedicated purely to mediation on behalf of the people he came to save.

A phrase that is easy to pass over in 5:2 is the reference to those with whom even the earthly high priests are able to deal gently: the "ignorant and wayward." Who would that be? While there is no reason to press every detail of this description as though it were an allegory, the reference is an apt enough description of the plight of humans. The Christians to whom Hebrews is addressed might not have thought of themselves in those terms, and we would rather not think of ourselves that way either. But once again, if we intend to read details of the text as keys to theological formulations, we should think closely about the implications of this description of the sinfulness of people. The emphasis here is on sin as the weakness of humans and their failure to follow the way of Christ, as opposed to emphasizing any sense of their inherent corruption or "depravity." This is consistent with a number of other references to the human condition in the New Testament, although some historic readings of selected texts have advocated a pervasive sense of "original sin."

Verse 4 of chapter 5 highlights the divine intention in Jesus' service to people. Again it is possible that the author could be contrasting the calling of Jesus with that of some of the earthly high priests. For more than a hundred years before the time of Christ and throughout the first century, the appointment of the high priests in Jerusalem was often of questionable legitimacy. Some Jews protested the political appointments, and whole communities such as the one that left the Dead Sea Scrolls separated themselves from the temple worship because they saw it as tainted. The temple and the priests who served it continued to be considered legitimate for a great many people, however, so we cannot be sure whether the author of Hebrews had this critique of the earthly priests in mind.

The prophets of the Old Testament provide another frame of reference that might have influenced the writer of Hebrews, as their calling by God was often an essential aspect of their identity. But in the time closer to the New Testament era, it was the priests who were considered to have been chosen by God through the succession from the priestly families ordained by God. And Jesus' calling as a priest was even more direct. The next section of the exposition of Hebrews

(7:1–10:18) will develop further the idea that Jesus' priesthood was modeled after that of Melchizedek instead of the Aaronic line of priests, but the point here is simply that his calling was from God. It was not like that of some priests who relied on political favors for their appointment, based on their own desire for the position and the benefits it held for them.

Unfortunately, it is still true in our time, not unlike the first century, that the genuine calling of some who call themselves ministers may be suspect. When the writer of Hebrews assures his readers that Jesus "did not glorify himself in becoming a high priest" (5:5), we can probably think of ministers who give the impression that perhaps their calling is based on a desire to glorify themselves. The attention they receive and the authority they command are persuasive and attractive incentives to which some ministers do not even realize they are drawn. But Jesus' whole life was a demonstration of his selflessness. And once again the writer turns to the testimony of the psalms (Pss 2:7; 110:4) to confirm that the calling of Jesus is from God alone.

The final verses of this section of the argument draw together the images of Jesus as high priest that have been presented to this point. The author refers to a time in Jesus' life when he "offered up prayers and supplications, with loud cries and tears" to God (5:7). We can't be sure exactly which incident in Jesus' life this refers to—perhaps to his agony in the garden of Gethsemane, but possibly another episode when he prayed to God. The significance of this remembrance of Jesus' life, however, is that it recalls an action that parallels what high priests did—praying on behalf of the people. So Jesus did actually fulfill a function of a high priest during his physical life, and in so doing demonstrated his sympathy with human weakness. But he also experienced suffering for himself, while remaining obedient to God (5:8-9), and he was called to be a high priest just as God had called Melchizedek (5:10).

A final observation on this section relates once again to words about salvation that might be taken by some as statements to be read literally as a guide to the development of doctrine. Although I have already argued that the images found in Hebrews are presented more for their persuasive power than as precise statements intended to inform doctrine, they warrant careful consideration if various texts of the Bible are to be presented as foundational statements of doctrine. In this light, the reference in 5:9 to Jesus as the "source of eternal salvation for all who obey him" once again suggests that the faith in Jesus that leads to salvation is not based on confessed knowledge alone, but on *obedience*.

This emphasis, which pervaded the exhortation sections discussed in chapter 1 above, seems to appear consistently throughout the letter.

Thus the author ends this section of his argument in favor of faith in Jesus. He has presented images of Jesus as brother and pioneer, suffering alongside of humans as one of them even while he could have remained in glory instead. The writer has developed the image of Israel rejected by God for her disobedience and denied a share in God's "rest," while the hope of that rest is still alive for all who will claim it "today." And he has pictured Jesus as a faithful high priest, sharing the sympathetic understanding of other earthly priests and yet maintaining a sinless life, able to mediate in an unparalleled way for humans with the God who called him into service.

STUDY QUESTIONS

1. Look through Hebrews and see how many ways you find Jesus described with characteristics of brotherly love.

2. If God had chosen to appear on earth in human form today instead of 2,000 years ago, what might be "fitting" ways to appear and to mediate between people and God? How would this person identify with people? How would this person demonstrate leadership of people?

3. Sketch out a time line to help you think about the argument of Hebrews 3:1–4:13. Date the line from about 1500 BC to the present. Put on the time line the time of Moses and the Israelites in the wilderness (around the thirteenth century BC); the time of the psalmist (anywhere from the time of David, around 1000 BC to the restoration of Israel in the fifth century BC); the early Christian period when Hebrews was penned (mid-first to mid-second century AD), and the present time. Consider (1) what Israel did; (2) the psalmist's challenge for "today" based on his reflection on Israel's disobedience and God's response; (3) the writer of Hebrews' reuse of the psalmist's challenge for "today"; and (4) the significance of this challenge for readers today.

4. Based on a careful reading of the surrounding verses, why is the "word of God" referred to in Hebrews 4:12 as "living and active, sharper than any two-edged sword"?

5. What do you think it would have been like to be a priest in the time of Jesus and the early church?

6. Can you think of leaders who have inspired you by sympathizing with your problems and by having experienced life's difficulties for themselves and who seem truly called by God to lead in ministry? Can you imagine Jesus being like those people, only without any sin?

7. Look at Psalm 2:7 and Psalm 110:4. Can you suggest ways these psalms could be referring to someone other than Jesus? Can you see how the author of Hebrews interprets them in Hebrews 5:5-6 to refer to Jesus?

8. In what ways is Jesus shown here in Hebrews 5 to be superior to the earthly priests?

FOR INDIVIDUAL STUDY

If you are using this book to study Hebrews apart from a study group, start your study of this section by observing how it fits into the larger development of the sermon. This section of the text provides the first major development of the argument of the letter. It may be helpful for you to outline the argument through this section or to sketch it out in a series of pictures that shows each image the author presents. The study prompts above should give you additional guidance for focusing on the important ideas in this section.

Chapter Three

A BETTER COVENANT
THROUGH CHRIST

In chapter 1, we examined the opening and closing sections of Hebrews along with the direct exhortations from the author to the readers, placed at strategic points within the letter. In chapter 2, we began to explore the elaborate argument the author lays out to persuade his readers of both the advantage and the necessity of following Christ. This argument is laid out in three major sections, the first of which is found in Hebrews 2:10–5:10 and which emphasizes Jesus' suffering in solidarity with people and introduces the image of Jesus as high priest. It also highlights the choice that lies with people to respond to God and have eternal rest with God or to reject God and be denied that rest.

In this chapter, we will examine the second major section of the argument laid out by the author of Hebrews. This section of the argument continues the development of the comparisons between the earthly institution of the high priesthood and the priesthood fulfilled by Jesus and also offers a broader comparison between the old covenant that guided Israel and the new covenant that emerges in the saving work of Jesus. As was the case in the previous section, this section of the argument includes many images from the Old Testament and the traditions of Israel. These images provide categories for understanding what Jesus was all about. At the time Hebrews was written, these images would have been familiar to the readers. For us, however, there is sometimes a need to explain the images with which Jesus is compared from the history of Jewish worship before we can make sense of exactly what the work of Jesus means.

The outline below provides a summary of some of the topics this section will address (in bold), along with an idea of how this section fits in with the rest of the sermon to the Hebrews.

The first section of exposition (or argument) ends with two brief references to Jesus as a priest "according to the order of Melchizedek" (5:6, 10). The first section of exhortation likewise ends with this exact same description of Jesus (6:20). Obviously, this reference to Melchizedek is important for understanding who Jesus is, and so the second section of exposition resumes the development of the argument at that point. Hebrews 7:1–8:5 addresses a number of issues related to the high priesthood and uses Melchizedek to provide a frame of reference for the claim that Jesus is a better high priest than the earthly priests. The remainder of this section of argument addresses other aspects of the old covenant, such as the temple and the ritual worship offered there, particularly the sacrifices offered to God. All of these will be shown as inferior in light of the new covenant established by God through Jesus.

Along with references to imagery from the Jewish Scriptures, the author develops the argument with clever wordplay and strategies of persuasion that were common in speeches by other Greek writers of the time. The result is not a step-by-step proof of the superiority of the priesthood of Jesus and the new covenant, as much as our modern minds would appreciate such an approach.

Instead, we are left with a series of images and ideas that all bear witness to the wonderful way God chose to reach out to people through Christ. If the Scriptures had been written in our own time, perhaps the comparisons would have been to religious people and institutions more recognizable to our modern sensibilities. That is not the case, however, so we must try to put ourselves in the places of those earliest readers and imagine the world they inhabited. Then we can begin to see something of the fullness of God's grace through Christ and envision what it means in terms of our experience in the world today.

THE SUPERIORITY OF THE PRIESTHOOD OF JESUS (7:1–8:5)

The Superiority of Melchizedek's Priesthood (7:1-10)

Chapter 7 begins by introducing the story of Melchizedek. The author draws on the brief account in Genesis 14:17-20 of Melchizedek blessing Abraham as he returned from fighting to rescue his nephew, Lot. He finds a great deal of significance in seemingly minor details of the story and even fills in the story with information not provided in Genesis. All of these details become important because they allow for a comparison between Melchizedek and Jesus, and perhaps even more because they allow for a contrast with the priests descended from the tribe of Levi in Israel.

So in verses 1 and 2 of chapter 7, the author reminds us that Melchizedek blessed Abraham as he was returning victorious from his battle against the kings who had captured Lot, and he received an offering from Abraham. The author will find much significance in this offering, which he discusses at great

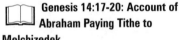

Genesis 14:17-20: Account of Abraham Paying Tithe to Melchizedek

The enigmatic character Melchizedek is described in the OT only in this brief narrative from the Abraham saga in Genesis.

After his return from the defeat of Chedorlaomer and the kings who were with him, the king of Sodom went out to meet him at the Valley of Shaveh (that is, the King's Valley). And King Melchizedek of Salem brought out bread and wine; he was priest of God Most High. He blessed him and said,
"Blessed be Abram by God Most High,
    maker of heaven and earth;
and blessed be God Most High,
    who has delivered your enemies
        into your hand!"
And Abram gave him one tenth of everything.

length in verses 4-10. But first, he finds important insights into the nature of Melchizedek in his name and in what he infers from a lack of information in the story about where Melchizedek came from. Melchizedek's name means "king of righteousness" in Hebrew. And since the story says he was from Salem, that makes him the king of Salem as well. Since Salem means "peace" in Hebrew, Melchizedek is the king of peace. So who could be more perfect in regard to these important qualities, righteousness and peace, than the king of righteousness and peace?

The Meeting of Abraham and Melchizedek

Here, Abraham is shown to the right, having just defeated the kings and is receiving a blessing of bread and wine from Melchizedek. The artist gives a priestly, sacramental focus to his interpretation as the bread and wine have a liturgical formality about them.

Dieric Bouts. c. 1415–1475. *Abraham and Melchisedek.* From the Altar of the Last Supper. 1464–1468. Church of St. Peter, Louvain, Belgium.

It doesn't take a professional linguist to recognize that this attribution of qualities to a person on the basis of his name is a dubious proof of character. And yet the argument developed by the author of Hebrews does not rely on sound principles of forensics. The argument is instead an artistic one, based on the flourishes of rhetoric and the cleverness of wordplay that the author uses to make associations and evoke images of Melchizedek's superiority.

Next, the author infers from the suddenness of Melchizedek's appearance to Abraham and the lack of any other reference to him that he appeared from nowhere. The story in Genesis tells us nothing of Melchizedek's past or his future, so it is possible to imagine him materializing fully engaged in his priestly persona and exiting just as mysteriously without facing death or the termination of his extraordinary priesthood. If we assume this kind of cryptic existence for

Melchizedek, we begin to see how the priesthood of Jesus can be seen as similar to his and how it can be regarded as superior in many ways to that of earthly priests.

Returning to the significance of Abraham's blessing and his offering to Melchizedek, the author weaves another image of the superiority of Melchizedek in 7:4-10. The earthly priests, here specifically designated as the descendants of Levi, were instructed to take a tenth, or a tithe, from all the descendants of Abraham. This would pretty much include all Israelites. But Melchizedek took a tithe from Abraham himself. Moreover, he blessed Abraham, and since blessings are always given by the person who is superior to one who is inferior, this means Melchizedek must be superior to Abraham. Not only that, but since Levi wasn't even born yet, you could argue that he was still inside Abraham (since ancient people thought babies originated from seeds that came exclusively from men). If this was the case, then in some sense Levi gave a tithe to Melchizedek too, even though he is the one known for his descendants collecting the tithes. All of these insights point to Melchizedek as a figure of importance and honor surpassing that of any of the patriarchs or holy men of Israel.

A Better Priesthood (7:11–8:5)

In the next verses, the author begins to use this model of Melchizedek to make direct assertions about the priesthood of Jesus. The reference to Jesus is subtle in many places, but we must not miss it. We can see it in the reference to "another priest" in 7:11 and 7:15 and "one who has become a priest . . . through the power of an indestructible life" in 7:16. Even though these verses do not refer to Jesus by name, they clearly refer to the priesthood he represents. References to "our Lord" (7:14) and to Jesus (7:22), along with the context of the statements made about this other priest, leave no doubt that the argument has shifted to an explicit comparison between Jesus and the earthly high priests. The basic premise of these verses is that the earthly priesthood was unsuccessful (as well as the law and the covenant as a whole), so it was necessary for a better kind of priest to come along and get the job done.

Some people might have objected to this depiction of Jesus as a high priest. After all, not just anyone could come along and declare themselves a high priest. Certain requirements had to be followed and criteria had to be fulfilled. That, of course, is where the comparisons with Melchizedek became vitally important. Melchizedek had been portrayed as a priest in the Jewish Scriptures, even though he did not meet the requirements established in the law. If he could be a priest, so could Jesus. And so the observations about Melchizedek that have been made so far are now introduced as precedents for the priesthood of Jesus.

First, perhaps the most obvious problem with the priesthood of Jesus was the fact that he was not from the tribe from which priests were required to come, the tribe of Levi. Instead, he was from the tribe of Judah. But the author, in 7:11-14, using the precedent of Melchizedek, turns this liability into an asset for Jesus. He argues that the failure of the Levitical priesthood made it necessary for a different kind of priesthood to emerge, one like the priesthood of Melchizedek. The most obvious change that could be initiated in the priesthood would be the calling of a priest from a tribe other than the Levites. So not only is it not a problem that Jesus is from a different tribe, it is *necessary!*

And the criteria for being a priest is further refined in 7:15-17, again with reference to Melchizedek. Instead of basing eligibility for the priesthood on physical descent, how about consideration of someone who is indestructible? Obviously, not many people would fit this description. But since there is no account of Melchizedek ever dying, he qualifies by this standard. And the author considers "indestructible" an appropriate description of Jesus as well. It is likely that he is thinking of Jesus' resurrection and his exaltation as indicators of his indestructibility, but he might also be referring to his incorruptibility. Throughout the suffering that Jesus endured, he never submitted to the destruction of his spirit or of his will. Either way, he represents a vastly improved candidate for the high priesthood. Psalm 110:4 is called upon in 7:17 as a witness to the fact that this high priest of the indestructible kind is a high priest forever.

Lest we miss the point, the author of Hebrews pauses in 7:18-19 to make it clear that this change in the high priesthood is very much to be seen as good news. Well, it's actually bad news/good news, but the good news greatly outweighs the bad. The bad news is that the old commandment is finally revealed to be weak and ineffective—the law ultimately didn't work. But this change, this new high priest to mediate for people, is the foundation for "a better hope."

Another affirmation of the priesthood of Jesus comes in 7:20-21 in the claim that the priesthood of Jesus was accompanied by an oath. The solemn oath of office sworn by the president of the United States comes to mind, or perhaps the oath taken by a witness in a court of law. Most of us likely don't think of oaths or swearing in this sense much at all. Jesus, of course, had harsh criticisms in the Gospel of Matthew for people who used oaths in a deceptive way to deceive people. But clearly the author of Hebrews saw an oath as a serious and appropriate validation of the priesthood of Jesus. The swearing of this oath is attested once again by the Jewish Scriptures, from the same psalm cited in 7:17 (Psalm 110:4) as testimony to the eternal nature of Jesus' priesthood. The author will return in 7:28 to this idea of the oath, arguing that the word of the oath has replaced the law as the authority for the appointment of priests.

In light of the oath that confirms the priesthood of Jesus, the author tells his readers in 7:22 that Jesus has now become the "guarantee" of a new covenant. The word "guarantee" probably conjures up associations for most of us from the world of commerce. We buy products daily for which there are guarantees, and perhaps we offer guarantees for our own work or products. Truthfully, I pay little attention to guarantees on small purchases. I may toss them in the garbage as soon as I have the product out of the packaging. But larger purchases, such as furniture, a computer, exercise equipment, or a car, make me much more interested in the terms of the guarantee offered. When more is at stake, the guarantee matters more. The state of our relationship with God is a critically important matter. This guarantee offers us most favorable terms. Perhaps more importantly, it's a guarantee backed by God. We all know that a guarantee is only as good as the person or company or institution that makes it.

The next comparison offered by the author between Jesus and the Levitical priests has to do with the continuity of their service. Levitical priests came and went. Because they were mortal, the death of one always meant the need for another to take his place. But the priesthood of Jesus goes on forever. Once again, there is no absolute logic that designates a once-for-all-time priest as better than a continuous line of priests in succession, but the author highlights the advantages and presents the contrast as one more image for the readers to consider.

The next image the text offers to the careful reader is a second claim that the incarnation of Jesus is "fitting." You may recall that in 2:10, the suffering of Jesus, his earthly life that allowed him to sympathize with people, was referred to as a "fitting" way for God to bring salvation to people. Here that word occurs again, the only other time in the whole sermon. But this time the emphasis is not on Jesus' earthly nature but rather on his transcendence as he took on the role of the high priest. It takes both of these emphases for the magnitude of the "fittingness" of Jesus to be demonstrated in full. Jesus would not have been a fitting savior if he had not been fully human because he would not have experienced what humans do. And yet he would not have been a fitting savior if he had not been fully divine because he would not have had the kind of access to the power and grace of God that allowed him to conquer sin and mediate for all people before God.

It seems likely that it was because of these two emphases, the humanness and the holiness of Jesus, that the author of Hebrews chose the figure of the high priest as a metaphor for the life of Jesus. It is apparent that the earthly high priests tended to fail both in sympathizing with their fellow humans and in being holy before God, but the ideal role they were to play offers a point of comparison for Jesus as he perfected both functions.

The emphasis on the sinlessness and perfection of Jesus that made his priesthood "fitting" brings the author back to a theme on which he touched briefly in 5:3. Since Jesus was sinless, he didn't have to offer sacrifices for his own sins. In reiterating this insight, the author connects it in 7:27 with two other highly significant themes. First, since Jesus doesn't have to offer sacrifice continually, he did it all at one time. This fact is undoubtedly offered as an advantage, and yet it has one alarming consequence that is highlighted in the exhortation sections of the letter: This offering can only be accepted on behalf of any individual one time. If a person accepts it, then rejects it, there are no more offerings to be made. Should this warning be regarded loosely for the sake of metaphor and rhetorical effect, or is it to be taken as a literal statement of doctrinal import? This is a difficult question, but keep in mind that the context here presents this once-for-all sacrifice of Jesus as a positive improvement over the way of the old covenant, and nothing in the letter suggests a capriciousness of God that would allow the "once-for-all" element to become a trap for people with a bad sense of timing.

The second theme that emerges in 7:27 is that the sacrifice Jesus offered as a high priest was himself. This theme will be developed much more fully in 9:15-22. It is mentioned only in passing here, but its significance is immense.

The final verses of chapter 7 and the first five verses of chapter 8 summarize some of the most important insights about Jesus as high priest. They also prepare the way for a broader comparison between the old covenant God had with Israel and the new covenant offered through Christ. Looking ahead to the developments that follow, the author begins to emphasize the idea that the old covenant represents a world we can see and touch, but one that is merely an inferior replica of the *real* world and the covenant that exists in the more genuine realm. This kind of thinking reminds us of the philosophy of Plato and his understanding that everything we experience in this world is somehow only an imperfect copy of real objects in another realm. The author of Hebrews speaks of Jesus' priesthood being carried out in "the sanctuary and the true tent that the Lord . . . has set up" (8:2). He refers to the worship of the Israelites as taking place in "a sanctuary that is a sketch and shadow of the heavenly one" (8:5). This perspective will pervade the next section of the argument.

A BETTER COVENANT (8:5–10:18)

Instead of focusing narrowly on the role of Jesus as a better high priest, this next part of the argument examines various aspects of the earthly covenant, temple, priesthood, sacrifices, and ritual. All of these will be shown to be a part of this earthly, inferior realm that is only a copy of the perfect, glorious realm of God. If the readers can imagine this other realm, the author invites them to commit themselves to God and to begin even now to participate in the superior life offered in that realm.

As you look at this section of Hebrews, you don't need to absorb every detail, because the images do not generally create an argument that has to be followed from one point to the next. Some units of the text have to be examined as a whole because they involve several different concepts that revolve around one word or one idea, but those units are basically independent of each other. They all go together, though, to create a larger image that is illustrated by each of the smaller ones. And they all have a common theme—what God has done in Christ is better than what God did before through the old covenant with Israel.

The Old Covenant (8:6-13)

From the perspective of the author of Hebrews, the fact that the old covenant was flawed is evident even from the words of the ancient prophets. The author quotes Jeremiah 31 to capture God's own proclamation about the need for a new covenant. Israel had failed to live up to her end of the old covenant and had strayed from God's commands over and over again. But God did not give up on Israel. Instead, God spoke these moving and compassionate words of hope. Because God is righteous, we might have expected God's pronouncement to be solely one of judgment on the people who had so many chances but repeatedly turned away to worship idols, practiced dishonesty, and failed to care for the poor and vulnerable people within their midst. But God instead focused on the shortcomings of the covenant.

We could safely assume there really wasn't anything wrong with the old covenant per se, since God was the one who initiated it in the first place. But the weakness of people in the presence of the power of sin made it clear that the covenant was not going to be enough to help people stay in an appropriate relationship with God. The people are not able to do justice to the covenant. As interested as God is in justice, however, it is the mercy of God that stands out even more in the response we see from Jeremiah 31. God makes a passionate promise of a new covenant, one that puts the law in the minds and hearts of the people. God will find a way to make salvation possible for people. One way or another, God seems to say, "I will be their God and they shall be my people."

The Old Sanctuary (9:1-7)

These verses offer a brief sketch of the sanctuary in which the rituals of the old covenant were carried out. The author does not provide many details here. That may be because he assumes his readers already know what a temple would be like, either because they were familiar with the Jerusalem temple or because they could generalize from other (non-Jewish) temples they had seen. But it also seems likely that he provides precisely the detail necessary to create the sketch of the sanctuary that he wants to leave in the mind of the reader. This sketch will be the basis of the imagery suggested in 9:8-14, and it is this imaginary picture of the sanctuary that is important to his argument, not any precise details of the historical sanctuary.

In this sketch of the sanctuary, the important point is that there are two separate tents, or perhaps two separate sections of one tent. All the priests can enter one of those tents, and the priests stay busy continually with ritual activity in that tent. But only the high priest is allowed to enter the other tent, the one called the "holy of holies." And he can only go into that tent under special circumstances: he can only go in once a year on a special day (the Day of Atonement), and he must have with him the blood of the sacrificial animal to

sprinkle on the altar. That second tent contained the
fabulous treasures of the Israelites—the golden
altar, the ark of the covenant with all its
golden gilding, other golden
artifacts and famous relics, and to top it all
off, the original Ten Commandments
themselves!

In the New Sanctuary (9:8-14)

The difference between the two tents described in 9:1-7 provides a basis for a
comparison between the old covenant and the new, the old system and the new
way established by the sacrifice of Jesus. In verses 8-10 the author refers to two
different time periods, which he calls the "present time" and the "time . . . to set
things right." These two periods are to be compared to the two different tents.
The present time is like the first tent, the tent that is less prestigious, less important. In this period the rituals of gifts and sacrifices, dietary rules, baptisms, and
other regulations are not enough to make people perfect.

The "time . . . to set things right," however, is associated with the image of
the second tent, the fabulous one with all the history and all the glory. This
"time" is the coming of Jesus as high priest, and his tent is one "not made with
hands." His special entry into the tent is not once a year, but once for all time.
And the most spectacular improvement Jesus offers is the sacrifice of his own
blood, not the blood of even the finest of animals. So Jesus is described here not
only as the high priest, but as the sacrificial offering as well. We can add one
more comparison to the many that have already been suggested: "If the blood of
goats and bulls . . . sanctifies those who have been defiled . . . , *how much more*
will the blood of Christ . . . purify our conscience from dead works to worship
the living God" (9:13-14)!

Notice that the author of Hebrews does not describe the death of Jesus in
this part of the argument as being necessary. Instead he shows how valuable the
blood of Jesus was. It was offered in a manner that was in some way similar to
the animal sacrifices traditionally offered by the Jews. But it was also infinitely
superior to those sacrifices. The shedding of blood is a costly sacrifice, and it is
"fitting" as a way of restoring the relationship between God and people.

Blood for Forgiveness (9:15-22)

In the verses that follow, 9:15-22, the author continues to make comparisons between the traditional system of sacrifice and the new covenant instituted by Jesus. But the focus in this section will turn to the significance of blood for bringing about the forgiveness of sins. Verses 15-19 contain a play on words that doesn't translate well into English, but we need to take a careful look at the wordplay to understand what the author is trying to say. His comparison between a will and a covenant is based in part on the fact that in Greek, the same word, *diathēkē*, can mean either one. In other words, the author of Hebrews is making a pun here.

In verses 16 and 17, *diathēkē* is clearly being used to refer to a will, the document people prepare to tell what they want done with their possessions after they die. The author calls attention to the obvious fact that a will obviously doesn't *do* anything until the person who made it dies. The death of this person who has made out a will, for the sake of the author's argument, is treated as being the same thing as "shedding blood." In verse 20 he clearly goes back to using the word *diathēkē* to mean "covenant," as he has used it previously in 7:22, 8:8-10, and in 9:4. Then in verses 18 through 22 he is obviously describing the covenant God made with Moses and the Israelites.

By putting together the two different meanings of the word *diathēkē*, the author comes up with this conclusion: If a *diathēkē* (will) requires that someone die (shed blood) for it to be put into effect, then the *diathēkē* (covenant) God made with the people of Israel through Moses couldn't have been put into effect without the shedding of blood (9:18). This also explains verse 15, which introduces this whole analogy: Jesus is the mediator of a new *diathēkē* (will/covenant), and those who are called receive the promised eternal inheritance (bequeathed to them in the will), since a death has occurred (making the will valid) that redeems them from the transgressions under the first *diathēkē* (covenant with Israel/will).

English translations of the Bible have a hard time representing this play on words. The King James Version uses the word "testament" for *diathēkē*, and the New American Standard uses "covenant," but neither one works completely because those words do not suggest both the idea of a will and a covenant quite as precisely as the Greek word. Most modern translations tend to translate *diathēkē* by the different English words that fit best in each context, so you would never know by those translations that the same word occurs throughout the passage. Some provide a footnote to point out the fact that one Greek word lies behind the idea of both will and covenant in the passage, but others give up on trying to communicate the pun.

Does this pun provide a convincing argument? By our modern-day standards of logic, not really. This may be an aspect of this sermon that we should think of as an illustration rather than as the working out of doctrinal statements. Maybe the author considered the fact that this word had two meanings to be a divine sign that the concepts could be tied together in this way. We may not agree, but we can appreciate the author's insights and his creative use of language. This passage adds to the rich tradition of biblical images that have been interpreted to help explain the work of Christ in dying for people on the cross.

Heavenly Things, Real Things (9:23-28)

The final verses of chapter 9 return to an emphasis on real heavenly things as opposed to their inferior earthly counterparts. We are reminded that Jesus entered the heavenly sanctuary, not a copy made with human hands (v. 24). We are further reminded that he removed sin by sacrificing himself "once for all at the end of the age," unlike the earthly high priest who has to go in "year after year with blood that is not his own" (vv. 25-26).

But all of this points us to a new revelation, one about the end of time. Here the author proposes a new way of understanding what will happen at the end of time. This new way is better than the way many people must have expected the end of time to come about. The old way of thinking about the end of time was that people die once, then face judgment. But Jesus changed that by offering himself as a sacrifice. He died once, but when he did he conquered the sin that leads to judgment. So when he comes the second time, his mission doesn't have to be for the purpose of judging sins. Instead, it will be a mission of salvation.

This teaching is exciting good news, but how does it match up with all the other traditions we know from the Scriptures about the end of time? End-of-time references are notorious for the variety of images they present. They frequently portray events and sequences of events that do not all fit together. Some New Testament images of the end times emphasize the role of Jesus in judging people (Acts 10:42 and 2 Tim 4:1, for example). But here in Hebrews the author seems to be contrasting the traditional expectation that Jesus would judge with the assurance that Jesus no longer needs to judge sinners when he returns to earth. Sometimes it is best not to take end-time images too literally or to weigh them against each other. Perhaps each has a message for us about the nature of God and God's faithfulness to us and all creation. We must not overlook the profound promise this statement offers. Christ is going to come a second time "to save those who are eagerly awaiting him."

Hebrews does not shy away from the subject of God's judgment. We have already seen stern warnings in the exhortation sections and examples of God's judgment on Israel in the exposition. But here in the climax of the argument, the author of Hebrews is more interested in describing the vastness of the grace of God demonstrated in the death of Jesus. God replaced the old covenant with the new way in Christ. This image provides the heartiest encouragement the author can offer, not warnings of doom. This vision of the end time is more powerful than any of those images of judgment and punishment for sins. It highlights the salvation Jesus has already accomplished by his death, the victory he has already won by his sacrifice.

Better Offerings (10:1-18)

The first part of chapter 10 offers yet another round of images that illustrate the superiority of the work of Jesus to the old covenant, all drawing on the witness of Old Testament traditions. The author has not yet run out of ways to make comparisons between the earthly covenant and the new covenant inaugurated by Christ. Some of them seem a little redundant, but they offer a few new emphases as well.

Verses 1-9 pick up once again on the contrast between the realm of the "real" things and the inferior earthly realm. The author describes the law as only a "shadow" of "the good things to come." He points out that the law is unable to make people perfect. As he has stated before, he reminds the readers that if "the law" were not insufficient, there wouldn't be a continual need to repeat the sacrifices. This time he calls in Psalm 40:6-8 as a witness. As we have come to expect in Hebrews, the words of the psalm are taken to be the words of Christ. They highlight the contrast between the old system of sacrifice and the new way in Christ, and they demonstrate Christ's fulfillment of the will of God by his devotion to the new way.

This psalm expresses a theme we find in many of the prophets, that God was not pleased with sacrifices from people whose hearts were not right. God often condemned the Israelites for bringing offerings when their worship was insincere and they weren't treating the people around them fairly or mercifully (Isa 1:1-10, Jer 7:21-26, Hos 6:6, and Mic 6:6-8, for example). For the author of Hebrews, this psalm now says all offerings made according to the ancient priestly system are inferior to the offering of Jesus' body.

The author also draws from Psalm 40 an emphasis on the idea that Jesus did the will of God. The words of the psalm promise that the speaker will do God's will instead of offering empty sacrifices that God does not desire. If this speaker is understood to be Jesus, the remainder of the psalm suggests he accomplishes this by his true faith in God and by proclaiming the good news of God's love and faithfulness. The psalm shows us that the contrast between following ritual observances to fulfill the law and offering true faith in God is an ancient one. For the author of Hebrews, the sacrifice of Jesus offers a final and permanent response, a superior way of doing God's will for all time.

In verses 10-18, the author returns once more to the problem of the priests having to offer sacrifice over and over again. He cites Psalm 110 as a witness to the fact that Jesus already "sat down at the right hand of God." Presumably we are to take this to mean that once he has sat down, he is finished offering sacrifice. His single offering was all that was needed.

In case we need any more persuasion on this matter, the author offers one more witness, this time returning to the images of Jeremiah 31, which he first introduced in chapter 8. The focus now is purely on the new covenant and its exceeding value. He cites again the moving and hopeful words of the prophet: "I will put my laws in their hearts, and I will write them on their minds." And writing to those Christians who need a reason to rekindle their devotion to Christ, the author offers from Jeremiah a profound assurance: "I will remember their sins and their lawless deeds no more." What Jesus has done has monumental implications for the readers of this sermon. Forgiveness is complete, and the sacrificial offerings of the old covenant have been rendered obsolete. How could the readers not be persuaded by this news?

STUDY QUESTIONS

1. Review the story of Melchizedek in Genesis 14:17-20. What impression do you have of this priest? Why do you think the author of Hebrews chose Melchizedek for comparison to help describe Jesus?

2. Make a chart to compare Melchizedek, the earthly priests, and Jesus. In how many ways is Jesus superior to the earthly priests?

3. In what way is the once-for-all sacrifice of Jesus good news? In what way could it be construed as bad news? Do you think the author of Hebrews thought of it in any way as bad news?

4. What is the meaning of God's promise to "put my laws in their minds, and write them on their hearts"?

5. Explain the pun in Hebrews 9:15-22 that illustrates the necessity of the shedding of blood for the forgiveness of sins. Do you think this literally demonstrates the "necessity" of the shedding of blood, or might it be better to look at it as one more argument that shows how "fitting" the role of Christ was?

6. How does the role of Jesus in the end times depicted in Hebrews 9:23-28 compare to the role described in Acts 10:42 and 2 Timothy 4:1?

7. Do you think there are things in which we invest our time and energy even today that are only a "shadow" of "the good things to come"? How might our efforts be transformed by faith in God?

FOR INDIVIDUAL STUDY

If you are using this book to study Hebrews apart from a study group, start your study of this section by observing how it fits into the larger development of the sermon. This section of the text provides the second major development of the argument of the letter. It may be helpful for you to outline the argument through this section or to sketch it out in a series of pictures that shows each image the author presents. It may also be helpful at this point to go back and look at the exhortations discussed in chapter 1 and see how they relate to the sections of the argument that have been developed thus far. The study prompts above should give you additional guidance for focusing on the important ideas in this section.

Chapter Four

THE NATURE AND EXPERIENCE OF FAITH

The final section developing the argument of this sermon is found in Hebrews 11:1–12:24. In the first two sections we have seen the author develop a sweeping series of images that portray Jesus and his death as the centerpiece of a divine plan to allow people to experience the rewards of coming into fellowship with God. This plan provides a way that is superior to the way offered to Israel through the old covenants. Many parallels can be drawn between that old way of the covenants and the new way represented in the life, death, and exaltation of Jesus, and in every case the way of Jesus is better than the old way.

The focus in this final section of argument shifts, however, away from the faithfulness of Jesus to the faith of those who have already committed themselves to God. Instead of calling the readers to envision the work of Jesus and his role as a priest, the author here encourages them to imagine the reward already secured for generations of people who have trusted God. By reminding them of this multitude of others who have maintained their faith, many under difficult circumstances, he perhaps hopes to assuage the loneliness and isolation that have played a part in bringing the readers to the point of considering the abandonment of their own faith.

The outline below shows the major developments of this section of Hebrews (in bold), along with the larger context of the letter.

Introduction *1:1–2:9*
    Exposition 1: Glory through Suffering *2:10–5:10*
        Exhortation 1: Pastoral Assurance and Warning *5:11–6:20*
    Exposition 2: Access to God through the Sacrifice of Jesus *7:1–10:18*
        Exhortation 2: Pastoral Assurance and Warning *10:19-39*

FAITH DEFINED (11:1-3)

Chapter 11 begins with a famous description of faith. This notion of faith is important because there is no concrete evidence to prove that any of the images presented in the previous sections are true. No one can see Jesus offering sacrifice, no one can witness his high priestly actions, and no one can see with human eyes the reaction of God accepting the mediation offered by Jesus. And so it is necessary for Christians to be assured of all these things in another way. That way is faith.

In the previous sections of argument, the author has essentially constructed an alternate world for his readers to consider, an alternate understanding of what is real and what is ultimate. How can he convince them that they can already participate in this alternate reality, a world where God is triumphant and where God accepts them and includes them in the glory of an eternal place of rest? They live in a world where they feel persecuted and hopeless. How can they embrace this vision of a world where that persecution is overshadowed by peace and victory over sin because of the sacrifice of Jesus? And how can those of us who read this sermon today make the same leap from being mired in a world of sin and trouble to trusting in the sacrifice of Jesus to bring us into the glorious presence of God?

These are questions the author of Hebrews has framed by his earlier arguments, and he now presents a simple answer: by faith. Faith allows us to connect the vision of Jesus as the pioneer and perfecter of our faith through his own suffering with our own earthly existence. Both the stern warnings and the cheerful encouragements of the exhortation sections of this letter make it clear that the author wants most of all to persuade his readers to recommit themselves to faith in God through Christ. To this end he has offered a number of various images to help his readers see the world through different eyes. He is convinced that God has a plan of salvation far superior to any ever revealed before. But sometimes that salvation is hard to imagine for people living in this world. The other world in which we are supposed to have faith may seem distant and impossible to attain. So in this section, the author demonstrates that many others who have gone before us have followed the way of faith and have indeed found the assurance of salvation. We can be encouraged by their lives and their example of faith.

So what, exactly, is faith? We sometimes associate faith mostly with the content of what we believe. By this way of thinking, faith is "belief" in certain assertions, namely, that Jesus was God and that he died and was raised. But the author of Hebrews seems to present faith more as an attitude or a commitment that shapes people's lives. The examples of faith he presents in this chapter are all of people who lived before the death and resurrection of Jesus, so their faith obviously was not defined by those specific beliefs. Instead, their faith seems to relate more to their ability to live their lives in the hope that there was more to life than what they could see or experience. They all trusted God to give them a kind of fulfillment the world didn't offer.

THE ROLL CALL OF FAITH (11:4-31)

Abel

This list of the faithful starts with a character about whom we know little—Abel, the son of Adam and Eve. The story of Cain and Abel in Genesis 4 gives no explanation of why God considered Abel's sacrifice more acceptable than Cain's. But the author of Hebrews suggests that the reason God accepted Abel's sacrifice was because of his faith. We can only speculate on how Abel demonstrated this faith or how it was better than Cain's. In light of the message of the Old Testament prophets, perhaps we could assume that his heart was more devoted to God and that his offering was in some way more sincere than Cain's. Since the law had not yet been given, it would be hard to argue that Abel had earned any higher standing before God by keeping the law.

Anonymous. *Cain and Abel Sacrificing; Cain Kills Abel.* c. 1084.
Ivory plaque. Cathedral of Salerno, Salerno, Italy.

Genesis 4:2b-10: Genesis Account of Abel

Now Abel was a keeper of sheep, and Cain a tiller of the ground. In the course of time Cain brought to the Lord an offering of the fruit of the ground, and Abel for his part brought of the firstlings of his flock, their fat portions. And the Lord had regard for Abel and his offering, but for Cain and his offering he had no regard. So Cain was very angry, and his countenance fell. The Lord said to Cain, "Why are you angry, and why has your countenance fallen? If you do well, will you not be accepted? And if you do not do well, sin is lurking at the door; its desire is for you, but you must master it."

Cain said to his brother Abel, "Let us go out to the field." And when they were in the field, Cain rose up against his brother Abel, and killed him. Then the Lord said to Cain, "Where is your brother Abel?" He said, "I do not know; am I my brother's keeper?" And the Lord said, "What have you done? Listen; your brother's blood is crying out to me from the ground!"

It is ironic that the first person in this long list of the faithful is commended for the way he offered a sacrifice—the author has just spent several chapters emphasizing the inferiority of sacrifices offered by humans! Yet even in offering his sacrifice, Abel somehow demonstrated the faith God was looking for. Perhaps he gave a sacrifice that was costly for him, or perhaps he offered it with a more genuine devotion to God. For whatever reason, God accepted Abel's gift and recognized his faith. And even in death, Abel received approval from God.

One of the by-products of Abel's faith was a witness that continues to encourage people to have faith in God even though countless generations have passed. Verse 4 says "he died, but through his faith he still speaks." Death was not powerful enough to silence his testimony. Lives lived in faithfulness to God are never wasted. The fruit of those lives may not always be apparent, and they may even seem to be rendered fruitless by such an abrupt interruption. But every time Abel's story is told, his faith will be remembered and celebrated.

Enoch

The second of these heroes of faith is Enoch (vv. 5-6). We don't know much about Enoch, but he was a popular character in many stories written after the Old Testament period. No wonder he was a legendary figure; his claim to fame was that he never died. The author of Hebrews associates this grand exit from the world with his faithfulness. Whatever Enoch did while he was still on the earth, God was pleased with it.

Verse 6 offers an important observation about salvation. Perhaps as a further reflection on the faith of Enoch, the author says that without faith "it is impossible to please God." He goes on to describe the content of this faith by asserting, "whoever would approach him must believe that he exists and that he rewards those who seek him." This is a powerfully concise explanation of what faith is all about. And it is this rather broad description of the content of faith that informs the attitude of faith common to all the people presented in Hebrews 11.

As we read about the faithfulness of each of these figures and the approval God has given them, we inevitably wonder, "How did they all find God's approval without believing in Jesus Christ?" The answer seems clear for at least the people who made this list—they believed God "exists," and they believed "he rewards those who seek him!" This definition of faith connects believing and seeking in a fundamental way. The belief described in this statement goes beyond simple "knowing" in the lives of all these examples of faith. They don't simply know facts about God; they "believe" with a kind of confidence that leads them to commit their lives to seeking God.

This statement as a whole complements the statement defining faith in verse 1 and is (inversely) parallel to it. Believing God exists is nothing other than having a "conviction of things not seen," and believing God rewards those who seek God is having an "assurance of things hoped for." Both ways of stating faith are strikingly simple, and they establish the most basic common denominators for inclusion in the kingdom of God.

Noah

Again with Noah, in verse 7, we see that faith was essential for him to be saved from the flood. Noah's faith is also said to have brought condemnation to the world, perhaps because it put the rest of the world's lack of faith into focus. But most interesting in this summary about Noah is the statement that Noah became "an *heir* to the righteousness that is in accordance with faith." This kind of language seems to leave Noah's final reward still in the future. Whether the author of Hebrews intended to imply that or not is hard to determine. Paul similarly uses the language of inheritance in Galatians 4:7, although both in Paul and here in Hebrews it is impossible to know how far to press the metaphor. Still, it gives us language to help explain the relationship between the faith of someone who came before Christ, and perhaps even our own faith, and God's final consummation of the world and all the faithful in it.

Abraham

Far more attention is given to Abraham than to most of the other figures in this list of the faithful. From verse 8 through verse 19, the author tells the story and extols the faith of Abraham. Abraham is an interesting study in faith and must have been widely touted as an example of faith by the early Christians. Both Paul and the writer of the epistle of James appeal to the example of Abraham, although their emphases on the nature of his faith seem to be quite different, some would even say opposed, to each other. Paul contrasts Abraham's faith with reliance on works of the law, and James contrasts it with empty claims of belief.

Here in Hebrews, the author simply demonstrates the steadfast obedience Abraham showed, always with hope in the faithfulness of God. Bits and pieces of the story of Abraham emerge—leaving his home, dwelling in tents in a foreign land, offering up Isaac. Through it all he was able to see beyond this world to the other realm in which all the promises would be fulfilled. The author describes Abraham's vision of "the city that has foundations, whose architect and builder is God" (v. 10). Again in verse 16 the author says God has prepared a city for Abraham and these other people who demonstrated their faithfulness. This idea of a city prepared for the faithful is found in other Christian writings, such as the book of Revelation, but it probably also echoes the idealistic psalms that make reference to the city of God:

> There is a river whose streams make glad the city of God,
> the holy habitation of the Most High.
> God is in the midst of the city; it shall not be moved;
> God will help it when the morning dawns. (Ps 46:4-5)

> Great is the LORD and greatly to be praised
> in the city of our God.
> His holy mountain, beautiful in elevation,
> is the joy of all the earth . . . (Ps 48:1-2)

These psalms referred most directly to Jerusalem as the city of God. As we have seen so often in Hebrews, however, these images lend themselves easily to the vision of a world beyond the present world, as a new, ideal Jerusalem that God has prepared to await the faithful. In our contemporary traditions, we frequently sing of "Zion" not as the historical city on the mountain, but as the place where we will finally enter into God's rest. "We're marching to Zion, beautiful, beautiful Zion . . . the beautiful city of God."

Of course, Abraham never made it to that city during his lifetime on earth. Along the way, he received the fulfillment of some earthly promises, such as the inheritance of the land and the miraculous "power of procreation." But he still knew that the larger promise awaited him. All of the characters remembered in this chapter lived out their lives and went to their graves (except Enoch, of course) without ever coming into possession of the great promise of entering God's rest, but they never gave up on the promise. For Christians in every age it is important to remember that our lives consist of more than just the time we spend on earth.

So when could Abraham expect to finally arrive at the city God promised? It would be nice if we had a clear theological formula to explain the exact timing of everyone's entry into heaven and receipt of the promises of God. Even within the New Testament writings, Paul sometimes had to respond to people who had great concerns about those who died without having experienced the consummation of God's kingdom. In 1 Thessalonians 4:13–5:11 especially, we see Paul responding to Christians who were distraught because some of their fellow believers had died before the return of the Lord.

The author of Hebrews offers us not a clear theological formula, but a poignant image: the faith of Abel, Enoch, Noah, and Abraham was the kind of faith that allowed them to trust in God all the way to the end of their lives without receiving the promises, "but from a distance they saw and greeted them" (v. 13). Somewhere along the way in their difficult journey, I can imagine them waving as they see the confirmation of the promises of God to which they held so tightly. These people always believed God exists and that God rewards those who seek him. But the only eyes with which they ever saw those rewards were their eyes of faith, and even then from a distance. Still, they welcomed this vision.

The distance remained, though, and the other side of the joyful vision of God's fulfilled promises was the realization that their world was in some sense not home to them. Some people are uncomfortable with "pie-in-the-sky" expressions of faith, and no doubt they are sometimes expressed out of balance with other important dimensions of Christian faith. But Hebrews presents the positive aspect of contemplating our status as "strangers and foreigners on the earth." Clearly the author of Hebrews does not say we should hate this world or lose the hope of relating faithfully to the other people who share it with us. In fact, the opposite is true. The author calls for his readers to live out their lives with a confidence in God's faithfulness that allows them to love others and to do the will of God. He returns time after to time to admonitions about service and compassion toward others, about hospitality and purity and honor.

The author offers this vision of the world to come as a sign of hope. The point of looking ahead to the reward that awaits us is not to despise the world in which we live, but to help us endure it. Abraham and these others lived their lives on earth in a special way because of the hope their faith represented. The author of Hebrews wanted to encourage his readers to live their lives with a similar sense of hopefulness.

Isaac, Jacob, and Joseph

The author treats these three heroes from the generations of the patriarchs briefly, and they all are remembered for similar actions that demonstrated their hope in the future. Isaac and Jacob both passed along blessings to sons that would have meant nothing if they had not believed in God and the rewards God promised. Joseph's mention of the exodus was also a sign of his trust in the future God planned for Israel, a future in which God would always be faithful to reward those who sought God.

Moses

The brief recapitulation of the faith of Moses offers more fascinating details. As with Abraham, the faith of Moses is summed up with reference not only to one event, but a series of events from his life. The description of the first event is particularly interesting because it doesn't involve anything Moses did on his own. This great hero of the faith, perhaps the greatest in the eyes of the Jews, owed his survival in part to the faith of his parents. They were the ones who had the courage and ingenuity to save him. Faith in this instance was a community effort.

Then Moses himself made several choices that demonstrated his faith, choices that led to persecution he could have avoided by choosing differently. But his faith gave him the confidence to continue on in the face of persecution. Verse 26 offers a curious observation about Moses' faith, describing how he "considered abuse suffered *for the Christ* to be greater wealth than the treasures of Egypt" (my emphasis). It seems quite a strange statement to argue that the abuse Moses suffered was "for the Christ." But it is apparent that the author of Hebrews understands the faith "in Christ" as the same faith in God exhibited by people throughout the history of Israel. The kind of faith Moses had is inseparable from the kind of faith the author hopes his readers have. Moses could not have known of the life and death of Christ, the ultimate demonstration of God's grace. But he and the others who held on to their faith trusted that God would find a way beyond any already revealed to them to redeem them from this world.

Verse 27 returns to the idea that the sacrifice of Jesus and the new covenant offered by God belong to a realm in which we must believe without seeing it with our human eyes. The author tells us Moses persevered in the face of the king's anger "as though he saw him who is invisible." The invisible realm of God's existence and of the triumph of God's promises remains the theme of this discourse on faith. Moses had the vision of what is real beyond the world he could see, and he made the connection that allowed him to live his life with courage and hope.

The People of Israel and Rahab

The people of Israel, commended for their confidence crossing the Red Sea, and Rahab are the last in this list whose demonstrations of faith are narrated separately. Of all the people in the first section of the list, Rahab seems the most unlikely role model. She is, for starters, the first woman admitted to the list on her own merits. Sarah was mentioned in verse 11, but only as a potential obstacle to Abraham's faith that he managed to overcome. Undoubtedly, the culture of the Old Testament period was patriarchal. By the time Hebrews was written, the early church may also have already begun to revert back to patriarchal models after a start that apparently included women in important leadership roles. But the inclusion of Rahab in this list, against somewhat long odds, is an indication of the important roles women have played throughout the story of God's relationship with people, using their wits and their limited opportunities to the fullest.

Besides being a woman, Rahab also had history that we might presume would make her a less likely selection: she was both a prostitute and a Canaanite. The author does not make an issue of the fact that she was a Canaanite, but we do know that some of the traditions in the Old Testament called for the strict exclusion of outsiders, such as Canaanites, from the people of Israel. The author does, however, identify Rahab as "the prostitute," and we probably should see this as a double standard in reporting. The flaws of the previously mentioned men, some of them well documented in the Old Testament narratives, are not highlighted in any way. And the men who will be noted briefly in the more condensed summaries that follow are not remembered in such a way, or we would have a list that reads, "Gideon the idolator, Barak the hesitant commander, Samson the womanizer, Jepthah the child sacrificer, and David the adulterer/murderer." Still, the author identifies Rahab as someone who believed God existed and sought God. Her commitment to God allowed her to see beyond the walls of Jericho to another realm and to muster the courage to respond to her time of crisis with faith. By faith, Rahab *the faithful* did not perish.

THE WITNESS OF FAITH IN THE WORLD (11:32-40)

After these brief narrations of personal stories of faith, the author paints in broader strokes to begin to indicate the wide spread of the witness of faith in the world. The readers of this letter need encouragement, and the presentation of these examples of faith is meant to be a morale booster. The situation of the readers is perhaps reminiscent of that of Elijah when he fled from the wrath of

Jezebel and feared for his life. He complained that he was the only faithful person left in Israel, but God answered that 7,000 others would keep their faith even after the dust of all the political upheavals had settled. Likewise, the author of Hebrews, aware that the Christians to whom he writes feel a sense of alienation and loneliness in their struggle to remain faithful, wants to remind them of those who have gone before them and faced discouragements that were as bad as, and often much worse than, theirs. They are not alone.

The author makes it clear in verse 32 that these examples are only a sampling of the many stories of faith he could tell. He throws out a handful of names to encourage them, presumably of characters the readers would have embraced and remembered. This list is interesting at the least for its selection of figures. Some we might expect because of their significant stature in the history of Israel, such as David and Samuel. The others, all drawn from the stories of the so-called "judges," are something of a puzzle. The stories of Gideon, Barak, Samson, and Jephthah are unarguably some of the most entertaining stories in the Old Testament, and it may be that these larger-than-life figures enjoyed a status as folk heroes of a sort among the Jews and all those who revered the Scriptures of the Jews. Any critical reading of their stories, however, exposes considerable ambiguity and questions about their character. They were guilty of a number of indiscretions, from idolatry to sexual immorality to human sacrifice, not to mention bad judgment of various kinds. Even the book of Judges presents them within the context of a time when "all the people did what was right in their own eyes."

But the author of Hebrews highlights their dramatic victories and attributes their success to their faith. In contrast with the rest of the faithful listed in this section of Hebrews, who suffered for their faith, these legendary warriors were celebrated for their gaudy successes. Maybe the author wanted to show that not only many people but also all kinds of people have been a part of this great family of the faithful.

The remainder of the list lacks the names of specific individuals, although some of the descriptions of suffering perhaps evoke certain figures from various ancient Jewish stories. The women who "received their dead by resurrection," for example, sound like the widow of Zarephath (1 Kgs 17:17-24) and the Shunammite woman (2 Kgs 4:18-37), and reference to others tortured calls to mind the seven brothers of 2 Maccabees 7. These remaining descriptions tell of both great victories and horrendous suffering experienced by the many faithful in the past.

Chapter 11 ends by putting the faith of all of these people into perspective in light of the new way of Jesus. In spite of being "commended for their faith," not one of them received "what was promised" (v. 39). But all of these people have been described as examples of faith, role models to encourage the readers of Hebrews. Surely God has not rejected them. No, the author seems to suggest instead that all those who are saved, whether from before the time of Christ or after, will be saved through Christ and on a timetable that corresponds with the consummation of Christ's victory in his second coming. Verse 40 clarifies that they did not receive what was promised so that God could provide "something better." Again, this seems to point to the fact that Jesus' high priestly sacrifice will be effective even for these people who lived out their earthly lives generations before the coming of Christ, as long as they had faith in God.

So the author does not intend to disparage either the faith of the heroes listed here or their reward, but to show that even their faith is subject to the better way of Jesus. He couches this in such a way as to assure his readers that even these great exemplars of faith do not have an advantage over them. On the contrary, as the next chapter of Hebrews makes explicit, these giants of the faith provide a testimony to the God who saves them all. Readers can take comfort in knowing that if these people found God in a time even before the coming of Christ, they provide the final evidence of the assurance of things hoped for and the conviction of things not seen.

IMPLICATIONS OF THE "ROLL CALL OF FAITH"

Hebrews 11 is not a text that presents radical challenges to the broad framework of Christian theology. It is fair, however, for us to consider how the images of salvation found here fit with other biblical portrayals of salvation. While the whole list of the faithful celebrates lives lived in relationship with God, it takes little notice of boundaries sometimes considered sacred within Christianity. The "roll call of faith" introduces us to an earthy bunch of characters whose lives were full of ambiguity and who lived before the coming of Jesus. Some of them even lived before the giving of the law or God's choice of a people; their faith cannot be attributed to their obedience within the covenants established by

God for the chosen people of Israel. And yet they all found meaning in life because they believed in God and believed God would reward those seeking God. They lived lives of courage and lives that honored God. They help us know what it means to have faith in God, not in an analytical way, but in a creative way that captures our imaginations and invites us to be a part of their story.

SURROUNDED BY WITNESSES, JESUS AHEAD (12:1-3)

In chapter 11, the author has called to mind the many heroes of faith that have gone before, some by name and many more by allusion. Now he conjures up the whole crowd of them, and he describes them as surrounding the readers like a cloud. These readers have almost certainly felt demoralized and isolated, alone in this world and struggling to muster the courage and the will to follow the way of Jesus. But now they are encouraged to imagine themselves in a race, being urged on by this great fellowship of the faithful.

In some sense, the whole sermon is about imagination—not about make-believe, but about picturing real things we cannot see with our physical eyes. After all, how can we have the "conviction of things not seen" unless we can imagine what those things are? And what are "things hoped for" if not things we can imagine in such a way as to know they are things we long to have? The letter to the Hebrews contains a great many references to "seeing," and many of them have to do with seeing things that are not visible to us on earth. But if we trust our imaginations to the stories and images Scripture provides for us, we will be able to see beyond the limitations of our earthly eyes and minds. We will see every aspect of our lives in a different light—our relationships, our responsibilities, our use of our time and our resources, our attitude toward disappointments, our very definition of a successful life!

And the cloud of witnesses is only the beginning of the vision the author of Hebrews lays out in these first verses of chapter 12. If the readers are invited to imagine friendly faces on either side and all around, they are also invited to look ahead as they run for the ultimate encouragement, Jesus Christ. This vision of Jesus is defined by all the images presented in the various parts of the argument to this point: Jesus is pioneer and perfecter of the faith; he is the one who suffered, but now he is also the one who sits in glory at the right hand of God. This is the vision of what lies ahead for those who have faith. The author invites the readers to embrace the vision. This effect has been captured in our time in the simple chorus "Turn your eyes upon Jesus, look full in his wonderful face, and the things of earth will grow strangely dim in the light of his glory and grace."

OUTCOMES OF FAITH (12:4-17)

In verses 4-11, the author seeks to put the readers' suffering into perspective. He points out that their suffering is not as severe as it might be, at least not yet, since they haven't yet come to the point of bloodshed (v. 4). But he offers an understanding of suffering that sees it as neither a random consequence of life nor a kind of spiritual warfare. Rather, he describes their suffering as a redemptive process by which God disciplines them.

Drawing on the wisdom of Proverbs in verses 5-6 (Prov 3:11-12), the author suggests that they remember that they are children (literally, sons, but surely this image has meaning for both men and women today) of God. Everyone knows how persecuted children often feel when they have to do the things their parents feel are good for them—completing homework assignments, brushing teeth, eating vegetables, taking a bath, etc. No doubt children were no different in the first century. And children are not able to consider the long-term effects of their actions well enough to make sense of the (dramatic) suffering these kinds of disciplines bring them.

The author of Hebrews frames the suffering of his readers as a similar case of discipline in which God is the parent and the suffering Christians are the children who have a hard time making sense of it because they fail to see its long-term benefit. If his readers can imagine their hardships in this light, it will transform the way they deal with the hardships. Instead of thinking their difficulties are a sign of God's lack of concern or God's angry judgment on them, they will see trials as a sign that God loves them and wants to make them better people. Instead of assuming that these troubles mean they must not be God's people, they will see them as an indication that they are indeed special people to God. In fact, God only disciplines the ones God loves the most!

This positive outlook on suffering is by no means unique to Hebrews; it was evidently a part of the earliest Christians' coping strategy, necessary because suffering accompanied the spread of the gospel from the beginning. We must remember, however, that the suffering of the early church was persistent because of the people's unprotected minority status and their lack of religious liberty. Western Christians can only begin to imagine their situation. The author's explanation of suffering was a pastoral response to the people's circumstances. Christians today must make sense of suffering in various contexts. While the idea of suffering as discipline is helpful in some instances, it is not the only answer to all suffering.

James McClendon has distinguished between three different categories of evil suffered by Christians and all creation: (1) suffering from evil that appears senseless and inexplicable, (2) suffering as punishment, and (3) redemptive suffering (James W. McClendon, Jr., *Systematic Theology, Volume II: Doctrine* [Nashville: Abingdon Press, 1994], 174-75). The first two of these remain for us to agonize over, the first in the face of tragedies too horrible to attribute to God, the second with the realization that only God knows if and when suffering is a form of punishment. The understanding of suffering as redemptive, however, may help us make sense of the concept of suffering as discipline. In some sense, that suffering might be seen as sharing in the suffering of Christ, the kind of redemptive suffering that can ultimately be used as a part of God's greater plan to bring all creation into freedom from its bondage to decay (Rom 8:21).

Verses 12-17 of this chapter make a few suggestions as to what the readers might do to live out their new vision. Verses 12-13 recommend a new posture to go along with the new worldview. We can often read a person's spirit by the way they stand and sit, whether they are confident and at peace with themselves or discouraged and unsure. The author could almost surely see the Christian community to which he wrote slumping in dejection and wilting in resignation. If faith is the conviction of things not seen, the confidence of these Christians should be the visible result of their faith.

The admonitions of verses 14 and 15 call the readers to renew their commitment to peace and holiness. Peacemaking will involve the entire community, and the admonishment in verse 15 is concerned with harmony for the sake of any individuals who might be influenced negatively by bitterness within the community. The leaders of the early church frequently showed concern not only for individual piety, but for behavior that both reflected well on the church as a whole and fostered a special sense of love within the church.

In verses 16 and 17, the author offers one more image of warning against falling away from faith—an illustration of Esau. The author of Hebrews judges him more harshly than we find him judged in the Genesis account of his selling his birthright. The lesson in Hebrews is the finality of Esau's decision and the impossibility of him gaining back what he had lost. The readers should consider the possibility that their own renunciation of faith in God would result in similarly grim consequences.

THE CITY OF GOD (12:18-24)

In bringing his argument to completion, the author turns once more to a vivid contrast of images representing the old covenant and the new. With references to "a blazing fire, and darkness, and gloom, and a tempest, and the sound of a trumpet, and a voice whose words made the hearers beg that not another word be spoken to them," he evokes once again the image of the Israelites in the wilderness, coming to the mountain where the holiness of God kept them at a distance. Even Moses trembled with fear. But this is all a part of the visible world that the readers of this sermon are encouraged to let go.

In place of the old vision, the author offers once more the image of the invisible city that waits for the faithful. This vision includes not only the city of God, with angels prepared for a big celebration, but also the whole cloud of faithful witnesses. Greatest of all, the final vision of the reality the sermon's readers must make their own brings them into the presence of God and of Jesus who suffered for them. This whole section of the argument began with the discussion of Abel's sacrifice, but it ends with the acknowledgment that even the sacrifice of Abel can't hold a candle to the overwhelming sacrifice of Jesus, the great high priest who offered himself on the altar to redeem all people.

STUDY QUESTIONS

1. List as many different images as you can from the previous two sections of argument in this sermon. Remember that many of the images focus on ways of thinking about Jesus and on comparisons between Israel's old covenant and the new covenant.

2. What is the connection between faith and hope according to Hebrews?

3. How is the reality proposed by the author of Hebrews different from the reality that would have been apparent to his readers?

4. Why do you think the author chose each particular figure from the history of Israel to highlight as examples of faith?

5. Whom would you choose as your favorite examples of faith from (1) the Bible; (2) Christian history; and (3) your own Christian community?

6. How do you understand the fact that these Old Testament figures obtained God's blessing even though they lived before the time of Jesus? Do you believe anyone could have faith in God today without the knowledge of Jesus? Evaluate this statement in light of Hebrews 11:6: "It is possible for a person to please God by believing that God exists and that God rewards those who seek God."

7. Recall a time or times when you felt lonely as a Christian. Do you think the people cited as examples of faith in Hebrews 11 had similar feelings at times?

8. How important is the community of believers to our faith?

9. How might you deal redemptively with a circumstance of suffering you presently face? How might God's grace grow in you or in others as a result of your response to your suffering? How should the church as a whole respond when it feels like it is suffering persecution?

FOR INDIVIDUAL STUDY

If you are using this book to study Hebrews apart from a study group, start your study of this section by observing how it fits into the larger development of the sermon. Think about the arguments presented about Jesus, and consider how the argument shifts in this section to focus on the response to God in people from ages past that gives testimony to God's faithfulness. If needed, go back and familiarize yourself with some of the stories of these people from the Old

Testament. Consider how their faithfulness compares to the faith of someone today whose faith is based on belief in Jesus. Observe that the encouragement of the first few verses of chapter 12 refer back to these figures from Israel's history as well as to the depictions of Jesus laid out in the earlier sections of the argument. Finally, consider the admonitions offered in the middle of chapter 12 and how they both round out the argument and connect it with the final section of exhortation that follows. The study prompts above should give you additional guidance for focusing on the important ideas in this section.

GLOSSARY OF LITERARY AND THEOLOGICAL TERMS

Allegory—A literary comparison by which a story has a second meaning. Numerous details within the story, such as objects and people and actions, can be understood to have a meaning beyond the plain meaning of the story.

Apocalyptic—Refers to a cluster of images associated in Jewish and early Christian thinking with the end of the present age and the dawning of a new age of justice and perfection brought about by God. These images include signs of the end, such as earthquakes and supernatural disasters, and dramatic intervention by an agent of God. The images were often described in texts that told of the revelation of these coming events through dreams or visions.

Atonement—Making things right between sinful people and God. People are consistently unable to do this on their own according to Christian Scriptures, so this reconciliation must be based on the mercy and forgiveness of God.

Calvinism—A system of Protestant theology named after reformer John Calvin. Among the teachings of Calvinism is an emphasis on God's predetermination of who will receive salvation, referred to as predestination.

Christological interpretation—Understanding of Old Testament texts that sees in them explicit references to Christ. This is in contrast to understandings that see these texts as referring only to their own historical contexts.

Christology—Theological study of who Christ was and is. High Christology refers to an emphasis on the divinity of Christ. Low Christology refers to an emphasis on the humanness of Christ.

Covenant—A solemn agreement between God and people. In the Old Testament, the covenant was the foundation for the fundamental teachings of Judaism, the Torah. The covenant was initiated by God and was always a source of difficulty because of the people's failure to abide by it.

Docetists—People within the early Christian community who denied the humanity of Christ. They believed Jesus only *seemed* (Greek, *dokeo*) to have a physical body, but this body was illusory.

Epistle—A writing sent to a person or a group of people. Epistle usually refers to a formal letter, intended to convey an important message.

Eschatology/eschatological—Referring to the end of the present age and the theology of things associated with the end of time.

Eternal security—The doctrine that salvation cannot be lost once it is received.

Exordium—In classical rhetoric, the introductory section of a speech. The Greek term was *proem*. The exordium was used to prepare the audience to receive the speech and to understand it properly.

Exhortation—A communication intended to persuade the recipients to take action. In Hebrews, this is accomplished by the dual means of encouraging and warning.

Exposition—A systematic explanation or interpretation of some subject. In the case of Hebrews, the exposition is the argument explaining the meaning of the life and death of Jesus.

High priest—The highest leader of a religious movement. In the ancient world, various religious groups had high priests. The Jewish high priest had ultimate authority over worship at the Jerusalem temple as well as broad authority over Jewish life.

Hospitality—Providing travelers with food, water, and shelter. In the ancient world, strict codes of conduct governed the honorable exchange between hosts and their visitors.

Intercession—Acting to reconcile differences between two parties, especially acting on behalf of one party to make things right with another.

Levitical—Having to do with the Israelite tribe of Levi. The law of Israel designated that priests were to come exclusively from the tribe of Levi.

Melchizedek—A priest who appeared mysteriously to bless Abraham and receive a tithe from him in Genesis 14:17-20.

Metaphor—A figure of speech in which a person, thing, or event is called by the name of another person, thing, or event in order to make a comparison between the two.

Midrash—A way of interpreting Scripture frequently employed by ancient Jewish rabbis and often involving a highly metaphorical understanding of the texts.

Perseverance of the believers—Doctrine in Calvinist teachings that asserts that those who are chosen to be saved (the elect) must necessarily continue in faith and be saved because God alone has determined and brought about that salvation.

Plato—Ancient Greek philosopher who taught that there was a perfect world of "forms" or ideas and a world people can perceive but which consists only of imperfect copies of the "forms."

Priest—A holy person who officiates in the worship of a religion, offering sacrifices on behalf of the adherents of that religion.

Redemptive suffering—The acceptance of suffering as a way of overcoming evil and sharing in the suffering of Christ.

Rhetoric—Communication crafted to persuade by the use of proven techniques. Ancient Greek and Roman philosophers and leaders placed a high value on learning such techniques, which were applied first to spoken language but later influenced written works as well.

Sabbath—In Jewish tradition, the seventh day, a day of rest from work. This day of rest corresponded to God's rest from creating the world in Genesis 1.

Sacrifice—The practice of offering food or animals to the gods as an act of worship. The Jewish religion had extensive regulations governing such ritual offerings.

Sanctify—To make holy, pure.

Typology—A specific type of metaphorical interpretation that sees in Old Testament stories, figures, and images "types," or models, of things God would bring about later in the time of Christ.